CULTURES OF THE WORLD

Uganda

Robert Barlas and Yong Jui Lin

mc **Marshall Cavendish**
Benchmark
New York

PICTURE CREDITS

Cover: © blickwinkle/Alamy

Alexander Joe/AFP/Getty Images: 28, 32 • Audrius Tomonis: 135 • Ben Simon/AFP/Getty Images: 85 • Dr. Gilbert H. Grosvenor/National Geographic/Getty Images: 90 • Greg Elms/ Lonely Planet Images: 1, 5 • Hutchison Library: 17, 26, 38, 66, 91, 96, 97, 105, 113, 117 • Jason Edwards/National Geographic/Getty Images: 46 • Jason Laure: 58, 93, 95, 99, 115, 121 • Jose Cendon/AFP/Getty Images: 116, 118 • Marco Di Lauro/Getty Images: 72 • Mark Daffey/Lonely Planet Images: 69 • North Wind Picture Archives: 20, 22 • Oli Scarff/Getty Images: 33 • photolibrary: 2, 6, 7, 8, 10, 11, 12, 13, 14, 18, 34, 35, 36, 37, 44, 48, 49, 53, 54, 56, 57, 60, 62, 64, 68, 78, 82, 83, 84, 87, 92, 100, 103, 104, 108, 109, 112, 114, 119, 122, 124, 126, 129, 130 • Topham Picturepoint: 16, 25, 29, 89 • Travel Ink/Gallo Images/Getty Images: 76 • Trip Photographic Library: 9, 19, 24, 31, 40, 43, 59, 61, 65, 67, 70, 71, 77, 79, 81, 88, 94, 101, 102, 106, 107, 110, 111, 120, 123 • Walter Astrada/AFP/Getty Images: 39, 51 • William F. Campbell/Time & Life Pictures/Getty Images: 30

PRECEDING PAGE

Ugandan children at Fort Portal.

Publisher (U.S.): Michelle Bisson
Editors: Deborah Grahame, Stephanie Pee
Copyreader: Sherry Chiger
Designers: Nancy Sabato, Bernard Go Kwang Meng
Cover picture researcher: Connie Gardner
Picture researcher: Thomas Khoo

Marshall Cavendish Benchmark
99 White Plains Road
Tarrytown, NY 10591
Website: www.marshallcavendish.us

© Times Media Private Limited 2000
© Marshall Cavendish International (Asia) Private Limited 2010
All rights reserved. First edition 2000. Second edition 2010.
® "Cultures of the World" is a registered trademark of Times Publishing Limited.

Originated and designed by Times Media Private Limited
An imprint of Marshall Cavendish International (Asia) Private Limited
A member of Times Publishing Limited

Marshall Cavendish is a trademark of Times Publishing Limited.

All Internet sites were correct and accurate at the time of printing. All monetary figures in this publication are in U.S. dollars.

Library of Congress Cataloging-in-Publication Data

Barlas, Robert.
  Uganda / Robert Barlas & Yong Jui Lin. — 2nd ed.
     p. cm. — (Cultures of the world)
  Summary: "Provides comprehensive information on the geography, history,
wildlife, governmental structure, economy, cultural diversity, peoples,
religion, and culture of Uganda"--Provided by publisher.
  Includes bibliographical references and index.
  ISBN 978-0-7614-4859-4
  1. Uganda—Juvenile literature. I. Yong, Jui Lin II. Title.
  DT433.22.B37 2010
  967.61—dc22   2009046002

Printed in China
9 8 7 6 5 4 3 2 1

CONTENTS

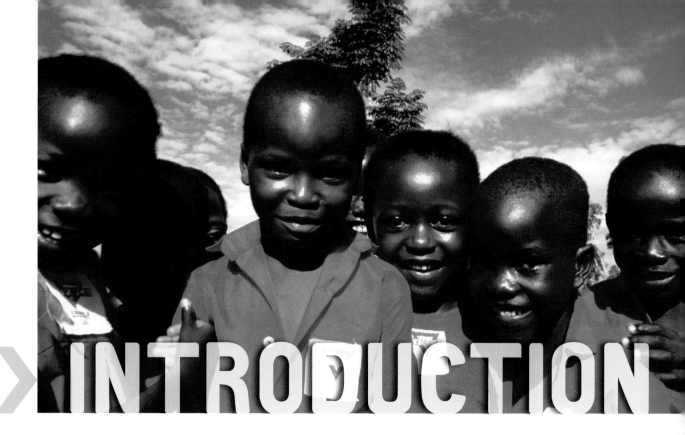

INTRODUCTION

T HAS BEEN SAID THAT UGANDA IS ONE OF THE MOST BEAUTIFUL but complex countries in the world. It is a young country—it became independent in 1962—but is home to several of the world's oldest cultures and to people of many ethnic origins speaking a vast number of languages.

Ancient tribal beliefs and customs still determine much of what takes place in Uganda, but they are now coupled with a modern, forward-looking optimism that permeates Ugandan society. Uganda's economy is still growing despite the global recession, and oil has just been discovered in the western part of the country, giving Uganda the potential to rank among the top 50 oil producers in the world. Its land is fertile, the literacy rate is increasing, and the people are determined to make the country work and prosper. It is a place with much potential for the future and a rich history in its past—and somewhere more and more people from other countries want to visit to learn about the cultural background of its very varied people.

Uganda also hosts the largest population of endangered mountain gorillas in the world, which along with its huge variety of flora and fauna brings millions of tourists. Furthermore, Uganda is at the forefront of global environmentalism, being one of the first countries in the world to ban the intrusive plastic bag.

GEOGRAPHY

The Murchison Falls along the Victoria Nile offers a spectacular sight.

CHAPTER 1

U GANDA IS 93,065 SQUARE MILES (241,038 sq km) in size and shares its borders with Sudan in the north, Kenya in the east, Tanzania and Rwanda in the south, and the Democratic Republic of the Congo in the west.

The western border with the Democratic Republic of the Congo runs through the Western Rift Valley, which is dotted from north to south by lakes—Albert, Edward, George, and Kivu. The tropical climate supports a vast array of beautiful flora and fauna.

The Ihihizo River flows through the Bwindi Impenetrable National Park in Kitaburura.

Situated right in the heart of Africa, Uganda is a small country with a remarkably diverse landscape, ranging from the snowcapped Rwenzori Mountains to dense tropical forests, freshwater lakes to breathtaking waterfalls. One of the relatively few landlocked countries on the African continent, Uganda is located between the two arms of the Great Rift Valley of East Africa.

Lush greenery on Mount Elgon. The climate varies throughout Uganda.

CLIMATE AND SEASONS

Overall Uganda has what is called a modified tropical climate, which is mainly mild and pleasant. But the climate varies a great deal throughout the country. Mean annual temperatures are about 79°F (26°C) in the southwestern highlands and 77°F (25°C) in the northwest, but in the northeast temperatures exceed 86°F (30°C) about 254 days a year. The hot climate is moderated by altitude; it is cooler at the higher elevations. Rainfall also varies from region to region. The rains are mainly from March to May and in October and November. Evidence of this can be seen in the changing landscape, from the dry savanna to the lush hills.

A TROPICAL PARADISE

Most of Uganda is lush and fertile, and the vegetation is extremely diverse, the result of the country's varied climates. Apart from the rather arid areas in

Uganda has three subclimatic zones, differentiated mainly by altitude and rainfall. The highest levels of rainfall are around Lake Victoria. The driest regions are in the northeast.

the north, Uganda used to receive abundant rainfall. Due to global warming, however, prolonged droughts, massive flooding, and hailstorms are occurring in Uganda with alarming frequency, disrupting agricultural production. Malaria is also on the rise due to an increase in temperatures.

The wild plants and flowers found in Uganda can be roughly classified by zones according to the amount of rainfall they receive. Much of the country's vegetation is in the flat savannas in the east and the northeast, while in the areas of high rainfall there are many trees typical of the rain forest. There is also a small area of semidesert in the north and the northeast, where drought-resistant bushes, grasses, and succulent plants grow. Evergreen trees cover a large part of the country, and there are rolling hills and meadows in the west. Much of southern Uganda was formerly covered by equatorial forests, but most of these have been cleared for human settlement.

Vegetation around Lake Bunyonyi. Uganda used to enjoy favorable rains throughout the year, but due to global warming, droughts, floods, and hailstorms are experienced more frequently.

The Rwenzori Mountains are an impressive sight.

HIGHS AND LOWS

Much of Uganda is a plateau, with numerous small hills and valleys and extensive savannas. The entire country lies in a cradle of mountains, with the volcanic Muhavura Range rising over the Great Rift Valley.

The Rwenzori Mountains are in the west, crossing the border into the Democratic Republic of the Congo and north of Lake Edward. In the center of the range, six peaks have permanent snow or glaciers. The highest of these peaks, and the third-highest in Africa, is Margherita Peak, which rises to 16,765 feet (5,110 m) above sea level.

On the border with Kenya in the east towers Mount Elgon, an extinct volcano and another of the highest mountains in Africa. Because of the gradual slope, climbing to the crater rim does not require mountaineering skills. On the wooded slopes great caves, gorges, and waterfalls provide some of the most exciting scenery in Uganda, and the terraced coffee plantations and bamboo forests enhance the wonderful views.

A LAND OF LAKES

Uganda can truly be called Africa's "land of lakes," as close to 20 percent of the area is covered by lakes, rivers, and other waterways. The largest of these is the famous Lake Victoria, which Uganda shares with Kenya and Tanzania. This is the largest lake in Africa and the second-largest body of freshwater in the world. Some of Uganda's other major lakes are Lake Edward, Lake Kwania, Lake Albert, Lake Kyoga, Lake George, and Lake Bisina. The lakes provide various attractions, such as swimming, sailing, and other water sports, and excellent fishing—Nile perch in Lake Victoria can weigh as much as 220 pounds (100 kg)!

Fishermen fishing on Lake Albert.

THE SOURCE OF THE NILE

The Nile is the mightiest river in Africa and the longest in the world. It originates in Lake Victoria and takes on different names as it flows through the country. From Lake Victoria it flows north to Lake Kyoga and Lake Albert as the Victoria Nile, but flowing out of Lake Albert, it joins the waters of the Albert Nile and then enters the Sudan, where it is called the White Nile.

White-water rapids and numerous waterfalls, such as the spectacular Murchison Falls, mark the Nile's course. Along most of its length the banks are thick with many varieties of plant life and home to waterbirds, and the more tranquil stretches provide watering spots for the multitude of game that inhabit its shores. Giant Nile crocodiles are seen at many points along the river, either basking in the sun or with just their eyes and noses visible as they float slowly along in the stream.

Victoria Nile through the rain forest near Kampala.

NATIONAL PARKS

Numerous national parks and game reserves provide a showcase for Uganda's vast array of wild animals and some of its most spectacular scenery. The parks display the extraordinary variety of the country's natural resources—freshwater lakes, swamps, mountains, forests, woodlands, rolling plains, and grasslands. To protect and effectively manage these invaluable resources on a sustainable basis, the Uganda National Parks department was established in 1952. It currently manages 10 parks.

The Bwindi Impenetrable National Park occupies 127 square miles (311 square km) in the southwest of the country on the border with Rwanda and, along with the 13-square-mile (33-square-km) Mgahinga Gorilla National Park (Uganda's smallest national park), is one of the best places to see some of the world's largest mountain gorillas—although it requires a lengthy hike to track them down!

Two men tracking gorillas in the Bwindi Impenetrable Forest, a UNESCO World Heritage Site.

Mount Elgon National Park is in the southeast of the country and surrounds Mount Elgon, an extinct volcano that contains a number of crater lakes. Mount Elgon is one of the best places to see the many varieties of Ugandan birds.

In the Kibale National Park, chimpanzees, monkeys, and beautiful forest birds are common. One of Uganda's most significant national parks, the Rwenzori Mountains National Park, provides some of the best, and most difficult, hiking opportunities in the country. Nearby is the Semuliki National Park, an eastern extension of the vast Ituri Forest, which is small but offers visitors two important attractions: refreshing hot springs and more than 40 species of birds found nowhere else in the country.

In the northwest lies Murchison Falls National Park, Uganda's largest national park, with its spectacular waterfalls on the Nile River. Along with Queen Elizabeth National Park and Lake Mburo National Park in the southwest, as well as the remote Kidepo Valley National Park in the northeast, Murchison Falls National Park provides some of the country's best opportunities to see big-game animals in the country. These parks are all flat savannas with plenty of wide open spaces in which the animals roam freely.

Hippopotamuses wallow in a river in Queen Elizabeth National Park.

UGANDAN MONKEYS

Uganda is one of the best countries in the world for seeing monkeys and apes living in their natural habitat. Members of the primate family found in Uganda include gorillas, chimpanzees, baboons, and velvet monkeys, as well as patas monkeys, many of which swing in the trees in the forests of the national parks. Black-and-white Rwenzori colobus (Abyssinian) monkeys are widespread in the highland forests and eat mainly leaves. The diet of other monkeys consists primarily of fruits and seeds. Gorillas can be seen near the borders of the Democratic Republic of the Congo and Rwanda.

THE ANIMAL KINGDOM

The biggest Ugandan land animals are the elephant, the rhinoceros, and the giraffe. Elephants are among the most impressive animals in the world and are present in most national parks, while the rhinoceros is among the largest species of animals in Africa and can be very dangerous when threatened. The best place to see giraffes in Uganda is Murchison Falls National Park.

Crocodiles, one of Africa's most awesome predators, are found in Uganda. They can grow to more than 20 feet (6 m) long. Although they are primarily fish eaters, they are responsible for more human deaths than any other vertebrate in Africa. Other reptiles include the rock python, one of the largest snakes in the world, and the African mamba, a venomous and aggressive snake.

Many species in the cat family can also be seen in the savannas in Uganda's national parks, including lions, leopards, wildcats, and cheetahs, one of the world's fastest animals.

MAJOR CITIES

Kampala, the capital city of Uganda, has a population of approximately 2 million people. Other major cities include are Gulu (146,885), Jinja (132,150), Entebbe (115,142), Mbarara (102,926), Mbale (84,100), and Masaka (75,391).

The crested crane is Uganda's national emblem and is depicted on Uganda's flag. It lives along lakes, swamps, and grasslands, where it can be found in large flocks.

Located on the northern shores of Lake Victoria at an altitude of 4,300 feet (1,310 m) above sea level, Kampala is the heart of Uganda. It is the largest urban center, the center of commercial life, and the seat of government. Today's forward-looking capital is vastly different from the battered city to which it was reduced in the 1980s. Modern buildings have sprung up all over the city, and old, dilapidated ones are slowly being renovated. Prior to Idi Amin's rule in the 1970s, Uganda had one of the richest economies in Africa. The mismanagement of Uganda's economy during the 1970s and 1980s due to political instability meant that there were fewer employment opportunities outside Kampala. This encouraged many people from around the country to move into the city, and most have not moved back to their home districts after the revitalization of the economy in the 1990s and 2000s.

Kampala is spread over several hills. Its origin goes back to 1891, when the *kabaka* (ka-BA-ka), or king, of Buganda had his court on Mengo Hill. The town grew to municipal status in 1950 and became a city in 1962. The climate of Kampala is typical of an inland tropical city. Temperatures range from a high of 81°F (27°C) to a low of 63°F (17°C), depending on the season.

Kampala, the capital city of Uganda.

Kampala is a vibrant modern metropolis adorned with gardens and parks. The Parliament Building and the National Assembly are in Kampala, as is Makerere University, the oldest and most prestigious university in East Africa. The National Theater is the most important place for cultural entertainment in Kampala, and people come from all corners of the city to enjoy performances of various kinds. The Botanical Gardens, founded in 1898, were originally natural forest used as a research center for the introduction of exotic fruits and plants to Uganda. Many of these fruits can be bought fresh in Kampala's Nakasero Market.

Jinja is a major commercial center and the third largest city in Uganda. It is situated on the banks of Lake Victoria at the source of the Nile, 50 miles (80 km) east of Kampala. Jinja is the home of the Nalubaale Power Station (formerly Owen Falls Dam), a magnificent example of modern engineering that supplies power to most of Uganda and parts of Kenya and Rwanda. Jinja is a good center for exploring the central part of the country, including the raging Bujagali Falls, located 6 miles (10 km) north of the city, and the source of the Nile 1.9 miles (3 km) away, with its monument to John Speke, who in 1862 became the first European to set eyes on the site.

The main street of the commercial center of Jinja.

HISTORY

Rock paintings at Nyero in southeast Uganda.

WRITTEN EVIDENCE OF UGANDA'S past goes back only 180 years. Arab traders first arrived in Uganda in the 1840s. King Mutesa I wrote a letter to Queen Victoria of England that was published in the *London Daily Telegraph* in 1875 stating that he wanted to be a "friend to the white people."

Nevertheless, oral traditions were important long before then, and from these much can be learned about what happened in Uganda several hundred years ago. Uganda has a long history, and the country seems to have been inhabited very early.

This wall was built to celebrate Ugandan independence in 1962.

Bantu people were engaged in agriculture in what is now Uganda from as early as 1000 B.C., and ironworking can be traced back to A.D. 1000.

During the 17th and 18th centuries powerful social and political orders developed, including the Bunyoro, Buganda, Busoga, Ankole, and Toro kingdoms, which made profitable links with the Sudanese slave trade that underpinned the regional economy. By the 19th century the kingdom of Buganda, the biggest area in Uganda, was allied to the powerful Shirazi of Zanzibar and gained control over the other, smaller kingdoms in the region. An hereditary *omulangira* (OH-moo-lang-gee-ra), or "hereditary king", ruled the Baganda people, advised by a *lukiiko* (LOO-chee-ko), Buganda's parliament.

KING MUTESA I OF THE BAGANDA

Although there were many tribes and people of different ethnic origins in the area that is now Uganda, for many years the kingdom of Buganda represented the real power in the land, and the king was the supreme authority with power over the life and death of his subjects. However, Buganda's history

Mutesa I, the king of Buganda, reviews his troops with Captain John Speke looking on.

Neighboring small states were happy to have Mutesa I as king of Buganda, for he often acted as their protector. Bwera, Kooki, Toro, and a number of regions south of Lake Victoria, for example, were Buganda's "protected states." Whenever Kabarega, the king of Bunyoro, struck at Toro, a rebellious part of his kingdom, the rulers of Toro and many members of the royal family received military aid from Buganda and even took refuge there. If there is a state in modern Uganda that owes its existence to Buganda, it is the kingdom of Toro.

also includes at least one king who was removed by his subjects because he was too cruel. The purpose of the *lukiiko* was to check the king's power. From its rise to power sometime in the 1600s until the third quarter of the 19th century, Buganda and its kings followed traditional ways of doing things, with very little interference from outside influences.

King Mutesa I was the last of the great kings of the Baganda tribe during the period of Buganda's dominance, and as so many changes took place so quickly during his reign, he was intuitively aware that he would probably be the last independent ruler of Buganda. The increasing numbers of Europeans, particularly missionaries, who were coming to his kingdom brought about the major decisions that had to be made during his reign. Mutesa I's greatness lies in the fact that he gave shape to the aspirations of his people by controlling and even being the architect of many of these changes. He enriched his country by encouraging trade with the Arabs and others and by peacefully opening up his country to new civilizations and cultures. There is little doubt that modern Uganda enjoyed its preindependence colonial status as a British protectorate very largely because of what Mutesa I had done.

Mutesa I's wisdom as a king was recognized far and wide, and many disputes were referred to him by his neighbors for arbitration. Many explorers, missionaries, historians, and colonial administrators who knew him well documented Mutesa I's personality as generous and hospitable.

When Mutesa I died in 1884, a fundamental change came over his kingdom. It was not as powerful as it had been. Though the people of Buganda

Captain John Speke introduces a fellow explorer to a tribal queen in 1864.

knew that things would never be the same again, the Buganda kingdom is still very much present and active in modern Uganda. Mutesa I was a good king. He died as a hero to his people and an international figure.

EUROPEANS IN UGANDA

In the 1830s Arab traders visited the kingdoms that constitute modern Uganda from their traditional bases on the Indian coast of Africa, shortly followed by British explorers looking for the source of the Nile, the first of whom was Captain John Speke in 1862. English Protestant and French Catholic missionaries arrived soon after at the request of King Mutesa I, and Baganda loyalties split into French (Catholic), English (Protestant), and Muslim parties.

JOHN SPEKE

John Speke, one of the early European explorers of the African continent, was born in England in 1827. After serving in the British army in India, he went to Africa in 1854 with another explorer, Richard Burton, where in 1858 they became the first Europeans to view Lake Tanganyika. Speke then traveled farther into the interior of Africa by himself, eventually coming across a large lake, which he named Victoria and claimed was the source of the Nile River. His assertions about Lake Victoria were not believed in England at first, so he mounted a second expedition to the same area between 1860 and 1863. He never got a chance to defend his claims a second time, as shortly after his return to England in 1864, he was killed in a shooting accident.

In 1888 the Imperial British East Africa Company was set up in Buganda with the king's permission, and in 1894 Buganda was declared a British protectorate. In 1896 the kingdoms of Bunyoro, Ankole, and Toro also became British protectorates, and the British extended Buganda's administrative system to these societies. In 1905 Uganda was put under the direct control of the British Foreign Office.

Uganda was never fully colonized, as non-Africans were not allowed to acquire freeholds—that is, to own land. By 1913, with the completion of the Uganda Railway, the cotton industry was well established, and by the 1920s, coffee and sugar were also grown commercially. Legislative and executive councils were set up in 1921. In 1961 a special constitutional conference on Uganda was held in London, and a timetable for independence was formally established.

UGANDAN INDEPENDENCE

During World War II, because the British were focused on defeating the Germans, Uganda was for the first time faced with the task of becoming as self-sufficient as possible. After the end of the war in 1945, the first Africans were nominated to Uganda's legislative council, and in succeeding years there was a steady increase in African representation. The success of

Mutesa I's successor, his son Mwanga II, became *kabaka* of Buganda in 1884. He was a weaker character than his father and became jealous of the power and influence the missionaries had gained during Mutesa I's reign. In 1888 his efforts to banish them failed, and he was deposed.

The colonial style of architecture of many of the old buildings in Kampala dates back to the short period in which Uganda was under British rule.

the council was undermined, however, by Buganda's participation; Buganda perceived a legislature as a threat to the degree of autonomy it wanted. This feeling was strengthened when Mutesa II was deported in 1953 for refusing to cooperate with the colonial government. He returned in 1955 as a constitutional ruler, but relations between Buganda and the protectorate government remained lukewarm at best.

In the late 1950s, with the emergence of a few African political parties, the African population concentrated on achieving self-government. The kingdom of Buganda intermittently pressed for independence from Uganda, and the question of the country's future became crucial. Finally discussions in London in 1961 led to full internal self-government in March 1962. Benedicto Kiwanuka became the first prime minister. Uganda finally became fully independent on October 9, 1962. In the general election held later that

The Ugandan parliament session on the day when the *Kabaka* of Uganda presented gifts to England's Duke and Duchess of Kent after the country's independence was formalized.

year, the Uganda People's Congress (UPC) gained the majority under its leader, Milton Obote. Obote began to act in a more and more dictatorial way, eventually abolishing the traditional kingdoms and proclaiming Uganda a republic. He remained in power until 1971, when a military coup was staged by former paratroop sergeant Idi Amin Dada.

IDI AMIN DADA

Amin was a member of the Kakwa tribe of northwestern Uganda. Lacking a formal education, he joined the King's African Rifles of the British Colonial Army in 1946 as an assistant cook. He fought against the Mau Mau rebels in Kenya from 1952 to 1956.

He was one of the few Ugandan soldiers to be promoted to the status of officer before Ugandan independence in 1962 and became a close ally

Idi Amin Dada in full military dress during his reign as Ugandan president during the 1970s.

of the country's new leader, Obote. The good relations he enjoyed with Obote, however, did not last, and in 1971 Amin took power following a well-planned military coup. He became president and leader of the armed forces and in 1976 declared himself president for life.

Amin's rule depended heavily on violence, and one of his most brutal acts was slaughtering a group of Obote's loyal army officers. One of his biggest mistakes was ordering the expulsion of Uganda's Asian community in 1972. He had not anticipated how destructive this move would be economically, as the Asian community provided Uganda with essential commercial expertise.

Murder, destruction of property, looting, and rape increasingly became the hallmarks of his troops. He also allegedly ordered the persecution of members of the Acholi and Langoi tribes. When he annexed Tanzania's northern territories in 1978, he found himself at war. Tanzania's troops defeated Amin's army, and his rule was over.

OBOTE VERSUS MUSEVENI

Ugandan forces exiled in Tanzania, including the Uganda National Liberation Army (UNLA), led by David Oyite Ojok and Yoweri Museveni, launched the invasion of Uganda that toppled Amin. The combined invasion forces were urged by Tanzania to unite and form an alternative successor to Amin's government. This brought about the formation of the Uganda National Liberation Front (UNLF) in Tanzania, with Yusuf Lule as leader. Barely two months into power, however, Lule was voted out of office and replaced by

In 2007, Uganda deployed soldiers to the African Union peacekeeping mission in Somalia.

Godfrey Binaisa, a former attorney general of Uganda. Binaisa was dismissed a year later by the UNLF military commission, and Milton Obote was proclaimed president for a second time in December 1980.

The second reign of Obote was disastrous for Uganda. There was widespread violence, including rampant murders. During the election campaign, Museveni repeatedly vowed that if the elections were not conducted fairly, he would wage war on Obote. True to his word, and starting with only 27 men, Museveni formed the National Resistance Army (NRA) and began a guerrilla war. Officers from the Acholi tribe eventually deposed Obote a second time. Another group, the Ugandan National Rescue Front (UNRF), composed of former supporters of Idi Amin and headed by Brigadier Moses Ali, formerly Amin's minister of finance, had also formed to oppose Obote during his second reign. After the fall of Obote in July 1986, more than 1,000 members of the UNRF joined Museveni's government. A peace deal was signed with the remainder of the UNRF in December 2002.

The NRA took control on January 26, 1986, and Museveni was sworn in as president three days later. President Museveni began a visible effort to build national consensus and promote reconciliation while dealing firmly with the remnants of the defeated armies. A National Resistance Council (NRC) was established with civilian and military representatives. This council developed and applied a system of committees throughout the entire structure of government, so that for the first time in Uganda's history, people were able to elect their true representatives, and there was a visible effort to maintain discipline among the military forces.

Museveni has been in power since 1986. In the mid- to late 1990s, he was lauded by the West as part of a new generation of African leaders. His presidency has been involved in the civil war in the Democratic Republic of the Congo (DRC) and other conflicts in Africa's Great Lakes region as well as in fighting against the Ugandan rebel group the Lord's Resistance Army (LRA). The LRA is a guerrilla army based in northern Uganda that has been guilty of numerous crimes including child slavery and mass murder. The LRA and the Ugandan government signed a cease-fire in February 2008 aimed at ending the long-running conflict.

Oyite Ojok, Obote's cousin, was killed in a helicopter crash during Obote's second rule, gravely weakening Obote's position.

GOVERNMENT

Supporters of Yoweri Kaguta Museveni cheering at his final rally before the elections in 2006.

THE PEOPLE OF UGANDA HAVE HAD many types of government during their long history, but until the coming of British colonialism and Uganda's becoming a British protectorate, there was no central government.

Originally the government was in the hands of the tribal groups, who elected their own elders and made their own laws, which all members of their group were expected to follow. Later some central authority was given to the kings of the various tribes, including the largest of these, the Baganda, whose ruler, the *kabaka*, was considered the king and had ultimate authority over his people and their land.

The entrance to the National Assembly Building in Kampala.

Uganda is a presidential republic whereby the president is both the head of state and the head of government. The government is made up of three branches: the executive, the legislative, and the judicial. Uganda runs on a multi-party system so that a broad spectrum of the people's interests are considered. All Ugandans aged 18 and above are allowed to vote.

Former president Tito Okello.

The Republic of Uganda is currently headed by President Yoweri Kaguta Museveni, who leads the National Resistance Movement (NRM), which has governed the country since the overthrow of former president Tito Okello in 1986.

MUTESA II

Mutesa II, whose full name was Sir Edward Frederick William David Walugembe Mutebi Luwangula Mutesa, was the ruler of the East African state of Buganda (now part of Uganda) from 1939 to 1953, and again from 1955 to 1966.

During the 1940s, although he was the king, Mutesa was essentially controlled by the British governor and was personally unpopular. He was advised on administrative matters concerning Buganda by his three regents: who consisted of the *katikiro,* or prime minister; the *omulamuzi,* or chief judge; and the minister of finance of Buganda. In 1953 when elimination of the privileged position of king of Buganda within the protectorate of

The legislative body of Uganda is the parliament, which is made up of 332 members elected by the people.

Uganda seemed imminent, Mutesa II took an unyielding stand in meetings with the governor of Uganda so as not to completely alienate many of his increasingly suspicious and anti-British subjects. His key demands were for the separation of Buganda from the rest of Uganda and the promise of independence. When he refused to communicate the British government's formal recommendation (which would have deposed him) to his *lukiiko*, or parliament, he was arrested and deported.

A KING IN EXILE

Buganda leaders engineered Mutesa II's return in 1955, as a constitutional monarch who still had a great deal of influence in the Buganda government. When Uganda became independent, Prime Minister Milton Obote hoped to placate the Baganda by encouraging Mutesa's election as president in 1963, but a conflict over the continued affiliation of the Buganda kingdom with Uganda followed. When Mutesa II tried to incite trouble between the traditionally stateless northerners and the southern "kingdom" members, Obote suspended the constitution. The conflict between the two men escalated rapidly. Eventually Mutesa II was forced to flee to Britain in 1966, where he died in exile three years later of possible alcohol poisoning.

A statue of Bugandan King Ronald outside the parliament building in Kampala.

NATIONAL AND LOCAL STRUCTURES

Uganda is divided into 80 districts, spread across four administrative regions: Northern, Eastern, Central, and Western. Most districts are named after their main commercial or administrative towns. Each district is further divided into subdistricts and counties. The counties of Uganda are divided into subcounties, which are further divided into parishes and villages. The head elected official in a district is the chairperson of the local council.

THE MAN AT THE CENTER

The current Ugandan president, Yoweri Kaguta Museveni, was born in 1944. His name comes from the word *abaseveni*, the local name for Ugandan servicemen in the Seventh Division of the King's African Rifles, into which many East Africans had been drafted during World War II. He was born in the countryside in Ankole, western Uganda, and because the peasants in his home area were nomads, he attended missionary schools when he was

Parallel with the state administration, five traditional Bantu kingdoms have remained, enjoying some degrees of mainly cultural autonomy. The kingdoms are Toro, Ankole, Busoga, Bunyoro, and Buganda.

Ugandans line up to cast their vote in the 2006 elections.

young. Very little health care was available to the Ankole, who were nomads by nature. They were also exploited and oppressed by land policies, including ranching policies instituted by the British and supported by some local chiefs and later by some neocolonial politicians. As a result of his background, Museveni became determined at an early age to fight against political and social injustices.

In the government that succeeded Idi Amin, Museveni served briefly as minister of defense. After Obote rigged the general election in 1980, Museveni opposed the tyranny of the Obote regime. During the struggle, Museveni's troops achieved a very high level of leadership and managerial skills, as well as clear political and military policies. They also established excellent working relations with the civilian population in areas where they operated. After a five-year guerrilla war against the regimes of Obote and his successor, Okello, Museveni became president of Uganda on January 26, 1986. He formed a broad-based government in which formerly hostile factions were brought under the unifying influence of the NRM. His reading of liberal Western thinkers such as Canadian-American economist John Kenneth Galbraith shaped his intellectual and political outlook.

UK prime minister Gordon Brown (*right*) with President Museveni (*left*).

The president appoints a prime minister, currently Apolo Nsibambi, who aids him in governing.

ECONOMY

A woman selling her produce at the twice-weekly market at Kisoro.

ENDOWED WITH SIGNIFICANT natural resources, including ample fertile land, regular rainfall, and mineral deposits, Uganda has great economic potential.

After the turmoil of the Amin era, the country began a program of economic recovery in 1981 that received considerable foreign assistance. As of 2009, Uganda looked set to beat the trend of the global recession with a growth rate of 7 percent.

Much of this reflects the discovery of oil in western Uganda, which has boosted investor interest in the country. The Ugandan economy is also

Workers picking tea teaves on a tea estate in the Rwenzori Mountains.

The political turmoil that has plagued Uganda has hampered its economic progress and prevented it from fulfilling its economic potential. Agriculture is an important component of the economy, creating jobs and generating revenue from exports. Tourism is another developing area, as are fishing and mining.

well positioned to meet the challenges it shares with many other countries in the world given its low public debt, comfortable level of international reserves, and relatively sound banking sector.

AGRICULTURE

Twenty-nine percent of Uganda's gross domestic product (GDP) comes from agriculture, and agricultural products supply nearly all of Uganda's foreign exchange earnings. Uganda is Africa's second-biggest coffee producer (after Ethiopia), and the nation earned $388.4 million through coffee exports from 2007 to 2008. Uganda has an ideal climate and extremely rich soil for growing crops, although only one-third of the estimated area of cultivatable land is used. Eighty-two percent of Uganda's labor force is employed in the agricultural sector.

Terraced fields. Agriculture is an important component of Uganda's economy.

TOURISM

Tourism in Uganda is an important generator of foreign exchange, high-end employment, and investment. There has been increased investment in tourism, particularly in travel accommodation and related facilities. Adventure tourism, ecotourism, and cultural tourism are being developed. About three-quarters of Uganda's tourists are from other African countries. Kenya, which borders Uganda, is the biggest source of tourists to Uganda, responsible for almost half of all arrivals into the country. Visitors to Uganda can enjoy many outstanding attractions, such as the numerous national parks and game reserves that provide unsurpassed viewing of the varied animal and plant species. Other attractions include the source of the Nile at Jinja, where it begins its 1,864-mile (3,000-km) journey to the Mediterranean, the spectacular Murchison Falls on the Nile, and the famous Rwenzori Mountains, which provide challenging climbing experiences.

Uganda is one of only three countries where it is possible to visit mountain gorillas. The others are Rwanda and the Democratic Republic of the Congo. Mountain gorillas are Uganda's prime tourist attraction. The vast majority of these are in Bwindi Impenetrable National Park, with a few others in Mgahinga Gorilla National Park. Both parks are in southwestern Uganda.

Tourists navigating the rapids of the Nile River.

MANUFACTURING

Manufacturing accounts for 24.8 percent of Uganda's GDP, and the manufacturing sector has an important role in adding value to agricultural output, by producing food and beverages and developing local substitutes for imported goods, thus accelerating overall growth. The industrial sector has resumed production of building and construction materials, such as cement and paint. Domestically produced consumer goods include plastics, soap, cork, beer, and soft drinks.

FISHING

Fishing is of growing importance in Uganda. Lakes, rivers, and swamps cover 10.9 million acres (4.4 million ha) of the country—20 percent of Uganda's land surface—and fish contribute a high proportion of Uganda's protein needs. The private sector has taken a great interest in the fisheries and has developed facilities for fish farming, fish processing, and the export trade. In all areas outside the central Lake Kyoga region, fish production increased throughout the 1980s. The government has supported

Local men buy fresh fish on Lake Victoria.

several programs to boost fish production and processing. China managed the reconstruction of cold-storage facilities in Kampala in the early 1980s. Soon after that, the government established the Sino-Uganda Fisheries Joint Venture Company to exploit fishing opportunities in Lake Victoria. In 1989, Uganda's Freshwater Fisheries Research Organization warned against overfishing, especially in the Lake Kyoga region, where there was a 40 percent increase in commercial and domestic fishing activity.

MINING

Interest in Uganda's mineral potential has been increasing substantially since the country made efforts to improve its mining and investment regulation. According to World Bank figures, between 2003 and 2007 mining revenues in Uganda grew by 202 percent, from $550,000 in 2003 to $1.66 million in 2007.

Uganda's gold industry has seen a radical increase in gold production. Uganda exported $61 million worth of gold in 2004, 10 times what it was exporting in 1998. Uganda's gold production has increased largely due to deregulation of gold sales by the central bank. In addition, Uganda acts as a middleman from the sale of gold from neighboring Democratic Republic of the Congo. Gold contributes up to 30 percent of Uganda's export

A miner carries a container filled with rocks at the Kawanga quarry just outside Kampala.

revenues. In addition to gold, small deposits of tin exist in southern and southwestern Uganda.

ENERGY

Burning of renewable resources provides much of the energy in Uganda, and the government is attempting to become energy self-sufficient. While much of the hydroelectric potential of the country is untapped, the government's decision to expedite creation of domestic petroleum capacity and the discovery of large petroleum reserves hold the promise of a significant change in Uganda's status as an energy-importing country. The capacity of the biggest dam, Nalubaale Power Station (formerly Owen Falls Dam), is now 380 megawatts.

Uganda is highly vulnerable to oil-price shocks, as it imports almost all of its 7,000 barrels a day of oil from the Kenyan refinery in Mombasa, which in turn imports crude oil from abroad. Discovery of petroleum reserves in Uganda has been welcomed in response to rising oil prices worldwide.

The hydroelectric dam at Owen Falls near Jinja.

Since assuming power in early 1986, Museveni's government has taken important steps toward economic recovery. The country's infrastructure—notably its transport and communications systems, which were destroyed by war and neglect—is being rebuilt. Recognizing the need for increased external support, Uganda negotiated a policy framework paper with the International Monetary Fund (IMF) and the World Bank in 1987. It subsequently began implementing economic policies designed to restore price stability and a sustainable balance of payments, rebuild infrastructure, restore incentives for production through proper pricing policies, and improve resource mobilization and allocation in the public sector. These policies produced positive results. Inflation, which ran at 240 percent in 1987 and 42 percent in June 1992, was 5.4 percent for the financial year 1995—96 and 7.3 percent in 2003. Currently the government is creating jobs and providing stimulus to the economy through road construction and other projects to rebuild the infrastructure, including information technology.

Uganda is currently experiencing a huge deficit in electricity. A large percentage of Ugandans do not have access to electricity. Those who do have electricity experience frequent power cuts popularly called load shedding.

FOREIGN TRADE

Uganda's number-one export is coffee, followed by fish, fish products, and tea. The leading nonagricultural exports are gold, iron, steel, and electrical products.

Uganda's main export partners are countries in the European Union, followed by Kenya. Uganda's number-one import partner is Kenya, which acts as Uganda's port, as Uganda is landlocked.

AFRICAN ECONOMIC COMMUNITY (AEC) Uganda is a member of the African Economic Community (AEC). This organization of African Union states established grounds for mutual economic development among the majority of African nations. The stated goals of the organization include the creation of free-trade areas, customs unions, a single market, a central bank, and a common currency, thus establishing an economic and monetary union.

WORKING LIFE

Ugandan labor is plentiful, generally well educated, and English speaking. Although the country has one of the best educational systems in Africa, with reasonably well developed commercial schools and colleges, wages are low by international standards.

In fact, because of past inflation, official wages are inadequate to meet the rising cost of living. Wages and salaries paid in the private sector are generally higher than those paid by the public sector. Many wage earners are able to survive only because they have access to cheap food supplies that are generally plentiful most of the year.

An employer must contribute an amount equal to 10 percent of an employee's gross salary to the National Social Security Fund (NSSF), and an additional 5 percent is deducted from the employee's salary for the fund.

Expatriates can work in Uganda provided they obtain a work permit. Foreign enterprises approved to operate in Uganda are usually granted such permits for their employees, so long as the applicants are key personnel.

TRANSPORTATION

The transportation and communications infrastructure in Uganda suffered heavily during the period of civil unrest. Roads and railways were destroyed during the troubled times, and it has taken the country a long time to recover. Recognizing the importance of the transportation network to the economic development of the country, the government has now implemented a transportation sector rehabilitation policy.

The most popular form of transportation in Uganda currently are the motorbike taxis popularly called *boda bodas*. *Bodas* are a bit dangerous, as many of the drivers are inexperienced and drive recklessly. Other common modes of transportation include walking, special-hire taxis, minivans, and bikes.

Uganda recently hosted the African Economic Community Summit in Kampala. The signing of a historic agreement to create the African Free Trade Zone (AFTZ) was announced at the summit on October 22, 2008. This free-trade zone consists of 26 countries with a GDP of an estimated $624 billion. In size and capacity, the AFTZ would rival most other trade blocks.

The Civil Aviation Authority was established in 1991 and operates as an independent body. Renovation of Entebbe International Airport has been completed; 19 international passenger airlines and three cargo carriers serve the airport. Uganda Airlines Corporation went out of business in May 2001. It was replaced by Air Uganda, which is the designated national airline for Uganda. The company was formed in 2007 and began commercial flight operations on November 15, 2007. Air Uganda currently flies to Kenya, Southern Sudan, and Tanzania, and its fleet consists of three McDonnell Douglas aircraft.

Kampala's railway station is the central point for Uganda's railway network.

The railroad system has 771 miles (1,241 km) of track, and the only one of of Uganda's neighbors it links with is Kenya. In September 2007, however, it was announced that Uganda would get four new railway lines connecting to Southern Sudan, the Democratic Republic of the Congo, and Tanzania. The Uganda Railways Corporation (URC) provides passenger and freight services, and recently it has significantly improved its transportation market share in the region.

Most of the 1,118 miles (1,800 km) of the bitumen-surfaced highway network in Uganda has been repaired, and there is long-distance and local bus service to most towns and cities in Uganda and to many of the smaller rural areas as well. In addition, there are 2,983 miles (4,800 km) of all-weather roads and 12,676 miles (20,400 km) of unpaved roads.

Most of the major lakes in Uganda have ferry services that crisscross the lakes and link the small islands to the mainland. Lake Victoria is the principal waterway with commercial traffic. In conjunction with train services, the railway companies of Uganda and Tanzania operate train ferries on the lake between railhead ports of the two countries and Kenya. These ferries load rail coaches and wagons.

ENVIRONMENT

A male mountain gorilla in Bwindi
Impenetrable National Park.

CHAPTER 5

U GANDA IS A COUNTRY OF abundant natural resources and breathtaking natural beauty. However, major environmental problems in Uganda include overgrazing, deforestation, and primitive agricultural methods, all of which lead to soil erosion.

Attempts at controlling the propagation of tsetse flies have involved the use of hazardous chemicals. Toxic industrial pollutants threaten the nation's water supply; mercury from mining activity is also found in the water supply. Poaching of protected animals is widespread.

Endangered species that are found in Uganda, include the mountain gorilla, the northern white rhinoceros, the black rhinoceros, and the Nile crocodile. The economic benefits of Uganda's biological resources are estimated at $ 741 million annually.

NATIONAL ENVIRONMENTAL MANAGEMENT AUTHORITY

The main government department in Uganda that has the responsibility of protecting Uganda's environment is the National Environmental Management Authority (NEMA). It was established in 1995 to promote sound environmental management and the prudent use of natural resources in Uganda. Given such a lofty mandate, it is no surprise that NEMA works with a number of other agencies such as the Department of Wildlife Conservation in order to achieve its goals. NEMA has received

To deal with years of environmental misuse and neglect, Uganda has set up the National Environment Management Authority to promote sound environmental practices and to protect the country's flora and fauna. Problems that Uganda faces include: deforestation, air pollution, and loss of wetlands. One of the more serious problems is the pollution of its freshwater.

assistance from the United Nations Environment Program (UNEP) and the United Nations Development Program (UNDP) to implement a project called Poverty Environment Initiative (PEI). One of the objectives of the project is to raise awareness of the links between poverty and poor environmental management. For instance, soil degradation costs Uganda $625 million annually—11 percent of its GDP. Sadly this cost is borne by the poor in Uganda.

DEFORESTATION

Uganda's total forest cover has been halved in the past two decades. In 1988, forests covered 26 percent of the country. This was reduced to 13 percent in 2008. The country loses an average of 212,511 acres (86,000 ha) of trees each year. Most of the destruction takes place on private land, outside government-protected areas. Conservationists are calling upon the Ugandan government to write off parts of forests and reserves it cannot secure from encroachers but to protect the hilly and mountainous areas that can be saved. The forest

Large swaths of rain forest have been cleared to make way for farmland and plantations.

sector employs 850,000 people, and the total value of Uganda's forests has been estimated at $222.9 million. That is the equivalent of 5.2 percent of Uganda's GDP. The destruction of the forests is costing the Ugandan economy $1.8 million annually.

AIR POLLUTION

The poor in Uganda depend on biomass fuels such as firewood, charcoal, solid waste, and kerosene for their cooking and heating needs. These, sadly, are the leading polluters in poor households, be they urban or rural. Firewood and charcoal account for 88 percent and 6 percent respectively of Uganda's total energy consumption. Food preparation takes a lot of wood fuel due to inefficient methods of cooking. There have been calls for improved stoves and renewable energy sources such as solar energy to reduce exposure to indoor pollution. Women and children face the greatest risk because they spend more time near cooking fires. Meanwhile, outdoor air pollution in cities such as Kampala is getting worse because of the increase in the number of vehicles on the road. The number of vehicles in Uganda has quadrupled since 1971, and Africa has the highest rate of urbanization in the world. The lack of stringent emission standards in Uganda is not helping the situation.

WETLANDS

Uganda's varied wetlands, including grass swamps, mountain bogs, seasonal floodplains, and swamp forests, provide services and products worth hundreds of millions of dollars per year, making them a vital contributor to the national economy. Ugandans use wetlands—often called the country's "granaries for water"—to sustain their lives and livelihoods. They rely on them for water, construction material, and fuel and use them for farming, for fishing, and to graze livestock. Wetlands supply direct or subsistence employment for 2.7 million people, almost 10 percent of the population. In many parts of the country, wetland products and services are the sole source for livelihoods and the main safety net for the poorest households. Many of the wetlands have been drained for agricultural use, however. The encroachment of the wetlands is costing the Ugandan economy nearly $1 million annually.

POLLUTED WETLAND CROPS

Kampala has several wetlands, covering about 16 percent of the district. Some wetlands in Kampala have been turned into dumping sites for waste products from factories and garages. Furthermore, whenever it rains, additional effluents are carried into bodies of water. Even the major wetlands that are connected to Lake Victoria and Lake Kyoga have been heavily contaminated by both industrial and domestic waste.

When the pollutants get into wetlands where crops are grown, they are extracted and absorbed by the crops. Although it is illegal to grow food on some of the Kampala wetlands, the ever-increasing population in the city has

The wetlands along the Nile River.

forced some of Kampala's 2 million people to reside or farm staple food crops in the wetlands.

WATER

As a whole, Uganda has more than enough freshwater. The distribution of the resource is uneven, however, and increasing amounts are required because of population growth, urbanization, agriculture, and industrialization. Rivers and wetlands cover about 18 percent of Uganda's total surface. These include Lake Victoria, Africa's largest lake and one of the major sources of the Nile River, the longest river of the world. Almost the entire country lies within the Nile Basin.

Lake Victoria is a major source of water for Uganda.

WATER POLLUTION

The water level in Lake Victoria has been receding with dire consequences, including the need for additional investments to extend the water output supplying the cities of Kampala, Entebbe, and Jinja. Between 2003 and 2006 the lake has lost 99 billion cubic yards (75 billion cubic m), about 3 percent of its volume. The ever-increasing lake pollution that has affected the ecological health of Lake Victoria—a result of a rapidly growing population, a booming fish-export industry, the disappearance of several fish species native to the lake, and the prolific growth of algae, among other reasons—has raised serious concerns. The industrial sector is a source of water pollution in Uganda as well because of the discharge of untreated or partially treated industrial effluent into nearby water bodies.

WATER SUPPLY AND SANITATION

The Ugandan water supply and sanitation sector has made spectacular progress in urban areas since the mid-1990s, with substantial increases in coverage as well as in operational and commercial performance. The successful turnaround of the National Water and Sewerage Corporation (NWSC) has attracted significant international attention. As recently as 2004, however, 44 percent of the rural population still had no access to an improved water source. Rural areas generally have less access to safe water than urban areas do. Limited access to wastewater treatment also is an area of concern.

WASTEWATER TREATMENT AND WETLANDS

The record rains of 1997 destroyed 40 percent of Uganda's feeder-road network.

The NWSC operates two conventional sewage treatment plants, one for Kampala and another in Masaka, which carry out primary and secondary treatment. If its quality complies with the national environmental standards, the treated sewage effluent is then discharged into an artificial or constructed wetland or directly into the environment. Wetlands contribute substantially to wastewater treatment. For example, the Nakivubo wetland in Kampala is estimated to contribute about $1.7 million per year to the Ugandan economy, serving as a tertiary wastewater treatment plant.

RECYCLING

Like most other developing societies, Uganda has an immense challenge when it comes to excessive waste, especially in the urban areas such as Kampala. Haphazard dumping of waste

Ugandans gather at a water distribution point.

is prevalent across all cities of Uganda. The Living Earth Foundation, an organization that works with communities to resolve their environmental concerns, has set up an Enhancing Plastic Waste Collection Program, in which 15 community-based sustainable plastic collection businesses were set up, private partnerships between local communities and plastic recycling companies were established, and biodegradable plastics were promoted. So far 3.5 tons (3.2 metric tons) of plastic have been recycled.

PLASTIC-BAG BAN

As is the case with most other developing countries, plastic bags have become a terrible environmental threat in Uganda. Plastic bags can take between 15 and 1,000 years to break down in the environment. Once plastic bags are discarded, they are blown in the wind, washed into drains and watercourses, and eventually ground into the earth. Uganda is blessed with some of the richest soil in Africa, but around the towns and villages it is laced with plastic. A layer of plastic and contaminated soil has formed in many areas, with an impenetrable crust that stops rain from soaking through. It leaves water stagnating in pools gurgling with methane gas bubbles.

In Uganda's capital, Kampala, discarded plastic has combined with toxic waste-management practices to make the problem worse. Although Kampala has 30 companies dealing in solid waste management, the process is mired in corruption. Poor areas of the city receive no service, because it is more profitable for the companies to target wealthy areas for the user fees they collect to remove rubbish. Scavengers in the municipal dump of Kampala earn 50 Ugandan pence a day collecting plastic bags. Most plastic bags do not make it to the dump, however.

In the slums and shantytowns the plastic bags are breeding grounds for disease, as in the absence of running water and a sewerage system, people use the bags as toilets. They are called flying latrines because when one has filled them, one throws them as far away as possible.

From July 1, 2008, the government of Uganda banned the manufacture, import, and use of plastic bags thinner than 0.001 inches (30 microns). All other polythene was and still is subject to a whopping 120 percent tax. From early 2010, however, any person caught using any type of plastic bag in Uganda will be jailed for three years or fined $1,500. The government is suggesting the use of local materials, such as banana-fiber bags and papyrus baskets, as alternatives to plastic bags.

ENDANGERED PLANTS AND ANIMALS

CYCADS   The cycads are a group of very primitive plants bearing a superficial resemblance to palms, although they are not at all related. Fossil cycads from the Paleozoic period (about 240 million years ago) have many characteristics similar to the cycads of the present time, which is why the latter are sometimes called "living fossils." The construction of the Mpanga River Dam in Kamwenge District is threatening the cycad species *Encephalartos whitelockii*, which is native to Uganda and grows only in the Mpanga River Gorge.

On March 9, 2005, a Nile crocodile that was supposed to have eaten more than 83 people during the past two decades was caught alive in Uganda and transferred to a sanctuary. The giant beast weighed about a ton.

NILE CROCODILE The Nile crocodile is the largest crocodile in Africa. Male crocodiles usually measure from 11.5 to 16 feet long (3.5 to 5 m) and weigh about 1,100 pounds (500 kg). The bite force exerted by an adult Nile crocodile has been shown to measure 5,000 pounds-force (22 kN). From the 1940s to the 1960s, the Nile crocodile was hunted, primarily for high-quality leather, though also for meat and purported curative properties. The population was depleted so severely that the species faced extinction. National laws and international trade regulations protecting the crocodiles have resulted in a population resurgence in many areas. Sadly Uganda is not one of them, and the Nile crocodile is under threat of extinction there.

A Nile crocodile basks on the bank of the Victoria Nile.

RHINOCEROSES Uganda was once the only place in East Africa with both white and black rhinos. Early travelers down the White Nile saw herds of white rhinos grazing on the river's eastern bank, while black rhinos browsed singly to the west.

Both species were hunted intensively during the British colonial period. When Idi Amin came to power in 1971 there were around 100 white and 300 black rhinos in northern Uganda; by the time he was overthrown eight years later, Uganda was devoid of all but a handful of rhinos. Three years later there were none.

Happily, in July 2006, Ziwa Rhino Sanctuary took delivery of two female and two male southern white rhinos from Kenya. Ugandans welcomed the rhinos as a symbol of the recent stability and reconstruction of their country after more than 30 years of conflict.

MOUNTAIN GORILLAS There are two main types of gorilla, each with several subspecies. The mountain gorilla is a type of eastern gorilla species (which also includes the Grauer's—or eastern lowland—gorilla) that is found in Rwanda, Uganda, and the Democratic Republic of the Congo, with a total population of only about 700 gorillas. The most recent census of mountain gorillas in Uganda's Bwindi Impenetrable National Park—one of only two places in the world where the rare gorillas exist—has found that the population has increased by 6 percent since the last census in 2002. This is extremely encouraging news, as there are very few cases in the world of a small population of endangered primates increasing.

NATIONAL PARKS

BWINDI IMPENETRABLE NATIONAL PARK This ancient rain forest is home to roughly half of the world's mountain gorillas and has 90 mammal

Rapids along a river in Rwenzori Mountains National Park.

The Virungas are home to a large variety of wildlife, including about half of the world's critically endangered mountain gorillas.

In 1996 water-hyacinth growth began to create a serious environmental and economic problem on Lake Victoria. By some estimates, at one point the hyacinths covered 14,826 acres (6,000 ha) of water, still less than 0.1 percent of the lake. When the masses of hyacinths drift into Uganda's ports and coves, they keep fish under the plants, impairing fishing, and trap small boats in ports. The weed invasion has also been known to affect cargo boat and ferry transportation by fouling engines and propellers and making docking difficult.

species altogether, including 11 primates, of which the black-and-white colobus, with its lovely flowing white tail, is prominent. Gorilla conservation has been a particularly high priority in Bwindi, where well-trained guides lead small and carefully supervised groups of tourists who pay $375 each for a permit to see the gorillas. The efforts have provided some compensation for communities around the park that have had to give up their right to cut timber and harvest game from the protected forest.

RWENZORI MOUNTAINS NATIONAL PARK   The Rwenzoris are Africa's tallest mountain range, and their distinctive glacial peaks are visible for miles around. A variety of large mammals inhabit the lower slopes, but the Rwenzoris are notable more for their majestic scenery and varied vegetation. The trails lead through rain forest rattling with monkeys and birds and then through tall bamboo forest before emerging on the high-altitude moorland zone—a landscape of bizarre giant lobelias, towered over by black rock and white snow.

MGAHINGA GORILLA NATIONAL PARK   Located in the Virunga Mountains, Mgahinga Gorilla National Park has great biological importance because throughout the climatic changes of the Pleistocene ice ages, mountains such as these provided a refuge for mountain plants and animals, which moved up or down the slopes as the climate became warmer or cooler.

UGANDANS

A Ugandan girl carrying her sister.

UGANDA HAS AN ESTIMATED population of 32.4 million and a population growth of 3.6 percent per annum. This rapidly growing population reflects the country's high fertility rate, which at 6.77 children per woman is one of the world's highest.

Uganda's population is largely rural, with about 87 percent of the people residing in the countryside, but the urban population is growing at a rate of 4.4 percent. The population of Kampala was estimated to be

Many ethnic groups reside in Uganda. Found all over Uganda are the Bantu. The largest of the Bantu groups are the Baganda. Uganda is also home to the elusive pygmies, who live in the forests along the border of Uganda and the Democratic Republic of the Congo.

Ugandans carrying heavy loads of washing to the river.

Uganda is a country of many contrasts. Just as the rugged mountains act as a foil to the broad savannas, and the dry uplands contrast with the wetlands of the lakeshores, so do the contrasts among the various peoples of Uganda reflect the variety of their surroundings. This is well demonstrated in the multiplicity of cultures, traditions, and lifestyles, which means that there is really no single Ugandan culture. Uganda is a melting pot of many cultures.

The nation of Uganda is a result of the unification of several ancient kingdoms and many smaller independent societies. Nevertheless, from their ethnic origins, most of Uganda's people can be divided in four groups in terms of both their language and where the majority of them live. These four groups are the Bantu, the Luo, the Nilo-Hamitic, and the Sudanic.

A division is made between the Bantu south, where the Baganda, Basoga, Bagwe, Bagisu, Banyole, Basamia, and Kenyi ethnic groups live, and the Nilotic north, home to the Western Nilotes, known as the Luo. The Acholi and the Lango are the two largest subgroups of the Luo. The Bantu make up nearly half of the population. The Western Nilotes make up 10.8 percent; the Nilo-Hamitic, also known as the Eastern Nilotes, 6.4 percent; and the Sudanic 6.9 percent. As a result of colonial rule, power was concentrated in the south, and therefore the Bantu became the dominant force in modern Uganda.

2 million in 2009. Average life expectancy is 52.7 years—51.7 years for men and 53.8 years for women.

BANTU PEOPLE

By far the biggest ethnic group is the Bantu, who can be found in eastern, central, western, and southern Uganda and constitute 46.3 percent of the population. They were the first group to migrate to what is now Uganda from Central Africa. Originally the Bantu people were mainly hunters and gatherers. They are believed to have introduced agriculture to Uganda with crops such as millet and sorghum. Although they split into many tribal groups and developed multiple languages, the Bantu tribes share one important characteristic that makes them easily identifiable: The names of most of the Bantu tribal groups begin with the prefix *ba*.

BAGANDA

Buganda is the kingdom of the Baganda people, the largest of the traditional kingdoms in present-day Uganda. Of all the Bantu groups, the largest is

Ugandan women in traditional Bagandan dress.

Nilotic-language speakers entered the area from the north probably beginning about A.D. 100. The largest Nilotic populations in present-day Uganda are the Iteso and Karamojong cluster of ethnic groups, speaking Eastern Nilotic languages, and the Acholi, Langi, and Alur, speaking Western Nilotic languages.

the Baganda. This is traditionally a group with no fixed social divisions—any person of talent and ability can rise to a position of social importance. This does not mean that Baganda society had no social classes; quite the opposite was true. At the bottom of the social stratum was a class of people known as the *bakopi* (BA-koh-pee), or serfs, who owed their livelihood to the goodwill of the *baami* (BAA-mee), or chiefs, and the *balangira* (BA-lan-gee-ra), or princes.

Next were the *baami*, who were in effect the middle class in Baganda society. This status was not necessarily hereditary but could be obtained through distinguished services, ability, or royal appointment. The highest class was the *balangira*, the aristocracy who based their right to rule on royal blood. At the very top of this class was the *kabaka*, or king. Buaganda kings generally loved their mothers, sisters, and maternal relatives more

About 6 percent of Ugandans—the Lugbara, the Madi, and a few small groups in the northwestern corner of the country—speak central Sudanic languages. The speakers of these languages arrived in Uganda from the north over a period of centuries.

The Baganda and other Bantu people of Uganda still make cloth from tree bark.

than their brothers or other paternal relatives. Some even go as far as to say that the Baganda are matrilineal. Hence, the titles of *namasole* (NA-ma-so-lay), or queen mother; and *nalinya* (na-leen-ya), or royal sisters.

THE PEOPLE OF THE NORTH

The Nilo-Hamitic and the Luo are found in northern, eastern, and northeastern Uganda. Sometimes called the Lango, the Nilo-Hamitic can trace their origins to Ethiopia and are mainly pastoralists. Unlike the Bantu, the Nilo-Hamitic groups have developed characteristics that distinguish them from one another, such as speaking languages that are quite different from the original one they shared as a group.

The Luo, which includes the Acholi, the Alur, the Jonam, and the Japadhola tribes, migrated from southern Sudan. They live in western, northern, and

A modern Ugandan family wearing traditional Banyankole clothes.

Roughly 10,000 Ugandans of Sudanese descent are classified as Nubians, in reference to their origin near the Nuba Mountains in Sudan. They are descendants of Sudanese military recruits who entered Uganda in the late 19th century as part of the colonial army employed to quell popular revolts.

Pygmies in Semliki Forest hunting and gathering food.

eastern Uganda. The Acholi tribe was traditionally organized in chiefdoms, each under a hereditary ruler known as the *rwot* (RWOT). The *rwot* was a link between the living and the dead and offered sacrifices to ancestors on behalf of the people. The administrative structures of the Luo were similar to the precolonial kingdoms of Buganda, Bunyoro, Ankole, and Toro.

The Sudanic tribes of West Nile originated in Sudan, but over the generations their culture and language have become distinct from those of current-day Sudan. Under colonialism, the Lugbara language was encouraged in elementary schools, and as a result, this group tended to dominate the rest.

PYGMOIDS

Pygmoids are part of a group of people whose adult men grow to less than 5 feet (1.5 m) tall. The Pygmoids of Uganda live something of a Stone Age lifestyle. They traditionally live by hunting and gathering, and they do not have permanent dwellings, tending to be seminomadic, camping for a time where food can be obtained.

The Batwa, a pygmy people, live mainly by begging from and working for the Bahutu and Batusi people, as there is no longer much scope for survival by hunting and gathering because of increased population and encroachment on gathering grounds. The Pygmoids are ethnically related to the pygmies of the Democratic Republic of the Congo.

Baganda traditional attire consists of a bark cloth wrapped from the chest to the feet and tied around the waist with a thick belt. Called a kanzu *(KAN-zoo), the cloth is partly covered by another piece of bark cloth tied around the shoulders. Bark cloth is made from the inner layer of a tree's bark, a fibrous material that becomes more resistant and supple the more it is beaten.*

Once the bark has been extracted from a tree, it is stripped of any remaining wood and rough outer layer. The bark is softened, either by soaking it in water or smoking it over a fire, then spread across a large, smooth branch, and hammered with a thick piece of wood. As it is beaten, the bark expands. After the bark dries, it is dampened and hammered once more. It takes about two hours of hammering to soften a piece of bark enough for simple clothes to be fashioned out of it. Completed bark cloths are worn for a variety of ceremonies.

Arab traders introduced kanzus *to the country. Today many* kanzus *are made of cotton or linen. As the formal attire for all Baganda men, the* kanzu *is worn with a suit jacket or a sport coat.*

Pygmoids can be found in the districts of Bundibujo and Kasese, inhabiting the tropical forests of the Congo River Basin on the western Uganda—Democratic Republic of the Congo border, particularly in the parts adjoining the Ituri Forest near the Ituri River, which has its source in the Bulega Hills overlooking Lake Albert and the Semliki River. The Pygmoids are believed to have been the original inhabitants of the Rwenzori Mountain areas before the arrival of the Bantu. Their original home is said to have been the forests of the Democratic Republic of the Congo, and their language, which is unique to them, is called Kumbuti.

Pygmoid men and women dress in the same way. A belt is wound around the waist with a piece of bark cloth attached to it. The bark cloth is brought down between the legs and fixed against the belt in the front. It is not very common for the Bambuti pygmy people to put on clothes, however. They usually go stark naked, though occasionally some of them may be found with a brass-wire bangle.

LIFESTYLE

The sight of people carrying loads on their heads is a common one in Uganda.

CHAPTER 7

ALTHOUGH UGANDANS ARE becoming more and more similar through the influence of modern communications and increasing intermarriage between tribal groups, most Ugandans for the most part still practice a variety of lifestyles that depend on where they live and what their tribal tradition has taught them is important.

Much of the lifestyle of Ugandans in the villages has changed dramatically as a result of modern-day ideas brought in through the media.

A Karamojong homestead near the town of Kaabong.

The introduction of and exposure to media such as television and newspapers has led to a change to a more contemporary lifestyle. However, in the rural areas, most Ugandans still adhere to a traditional way of life. The family is considered the nucleus of Ugandan life, and men and women are considered incomplete until they get married.

Nevertheless, many traditional practices and customs remain evident in the behavior and attitude of many Ugandans, particularly in the more isolated regions, where allegiance to a tribe and its beliefs can be more important than being "modern." The family unit is the nucleus of Ugandan life in rural areas, and families live a very close-knit existence in small village communities.

HOMESTEADS

Traditionally among agricultural peoples, the residential pattern was one of scattered homesteads, each surrounded by its own arable land and some reserved pastureland. Round houses with wooden frames, mud walls, and grass-thatched, conical roofs were common throughout the region. Banana-fiber thatch was used in areas in which bananas were common. Economies were all essentially subsistence—each household raised its own food supply and made its own clothes and houses.

Typical Ugandan homestead-style houses in a village near Jinja.

Specialization, other than ironworking, was unusual, although some individuals developed skills as part-time artisans in addition to their normal work as potters, wood-carvers, bark-cloth makers, and herbalists. Each village had a specially recognized man who was selected from among the elders and acted as an intermediary between the villagers and the local tribal chiefs, in addition to settling village disputes. These traditions are still very much in evidence in the Uganda of today.

THE FAMILY STRUCTURE

Some kind of compound or family homestead was typical in almost every tribal village and is still the situation in many rural areas today. In rural areas each household is ruled by the family head, who lives with his wife or wives, his married sons and their wives and children, and sometimes his younger brothers, all within a single, fenced enclosure. Variations of this occur when

The Ugandan family unit is large and sometimes three or four generations live together.

brothers, and sometimes paternal cousins, live together with their wives and children, or when an influential man attracts close clansmen and their wives. Even when a man has only one wife, he often also has an additional separate house or at least a room of his own where he keeps his possessions and entertains visitors.

It is the moral as well as the economic responsibility for the family head to ensure the production of sufficient food for his household. The men clear the bush, while the women till the land. Men work together to build round, grass-thatched huts for shelter and barter among themselves and their neighbors.

WOMEN AND CHILDREN

The women of the house and their children were the traditional nucleus of the family and the center of domestic activity. Each wife had her own house, sometimes partly or wholly fenced off, or at least her own room in the large house. She also had the primary responsibility of household management,

A Ugandan woman bounces her child on her lap.

child-rearing, food preparation, care of the sick and elderly, and overall family health and welfare.

A wife usually also had her own kitchen hearth, where she cooked for all the family, and she often also had her own food store or granary. Older children sometimes had separate sleeping houses in the larger domestic groups.

Today Ugandan women living in urban areas have careers of their own and try to juggle a home life with the demands of a job. As in any modern Western society, this can put a great strain on domestic life, as few Ugandan men take on an equal share of household responsibilities. Uganda is one of the most difficult places for women to live, according to a study carried out in 2007. Women in Uganda seem to be relatively politically empowered but struggle in terms of educational attainment and literacy rates. Interestingly, 53 percent of Uganda's workforce is female.

BOYS AND GIRLS

In rural places, Ugandan boys are raised to grow up into responsible men, and in some tribes, they are initiated into manhood by undergoing the ritual of

Ugandan girls carrying jerricans of water. Girls have traditionally been raised to be good housewives.

circumcision. Boys acquire skills while working alongside their fathers, who train them in methods of herding, fighting, hunting, agriculture, and trade. If the father is a skilled craftsman, such as a blacksmith, his son learns the art by working with him. This helps explain why some skills, such as ironworking, "rainmaking," divination, healing, pottery, and other specialties, tend to be hereditary. For instance, the Okebu tribe are known for their ironworkers, and the Banabuddu of Buganda are known for their bark cloth.

Girls are groomed to grow up into responsible housewives. Their mothers instruct the young girls in the proper ways of cooking, basketry, pottery, child care, and other functions related to managing the household.

BIRTH

Traditionally, as soon as a Ugandan woman was married she was expected to conceive and to give birth within a year. If this did not happen, questions would be asked, and if it took longer than what was considered "normal," the husband was at liberty to marry another woman.

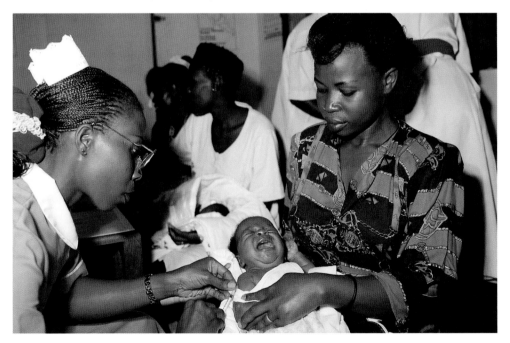

An infant being innoculated.

Today among the tribes, the more children one has, the wealthier one is considered. A woman is given more respect if she gives birth to a boy, because boys are the official heirs to their fathers. If a father has no boys among his children, he has to select an heir from his brother's sons.

Currently only 40 percent of women are aided by professional health workers when giving birth, and working mothers are usually given just eight weeks of paid maternity leave. Most women in rural areas give birth at home. After the birth the placenta is often buried, and the woman is confined to the home for a number of days. Sometimes she cannot even accept food from a member of her husband's clan until her days of confinement are over, although this practice is rare today.

Other customs associated with birth include confining a woman to the house until the umbilical cord has broken from the child's navel. The cords are sometimes kept in a special gourd, and the mother keeps the cords from all her children. In some tribes, women are also not allowed to look at the sky before the umbilical cord breaks off. A more extreme ritual involves killing a sheep by stomping on it until it dies to cleanse any taboos that accompany the birth of twins.

Some Ugandan women have children in their teens and become very young mothers.

The naming of a newborn child is done at a variety of times after the birth. Sometimes it can wait until the baby begins to cry continuously, but often the father, mother, or grandfather of the child names the child immediately after birth. Naming of the child also might wait until the umbilical cord falls off, at which time the names are given by the grandmother or aunt of the child, or even until after the third day, when it is named by the woman who helped in the delivery of the baby.

Some traditions even claim that an ancestor appears in a dream and dictates a name for the child—it might reflect the circumstances under which the child was born or be a day of the week, a place of birth, or the name of an ancestor.

MARRIAGE

The biggest tribal group in Uganda, the Baganda, regards marriage as a very important part of life. Years ago a woman was not respected until she was

Young Ugandans now opt for modern weddings rather than traditional ones.

One Ugandan tribe, the Alur, had a form of religious marriage. Tradition dictated that the man and the woman had to belong to the same religious cult to be socially accepted as a married couple. If they were not, the man had to be initiated into the woman's religion. If the couple subsequently divorced, the man would maintain the religious status he was given on his marriage.

married, nor was a man regarded as being complete until he was married. As the Baganda were polygamous, allowing a man to be married to multiple women simultaneously, the more wives a man had the more highly he was regarded in society. Today most marriages are monogamous.

In olden times, parents would initiate and conduct marriage arrangements for their children. Before the marriage, an important clan ceremony, *okwanjula* (ok-wan-JOO-la), would be held. In this ceremony, the husband-to-be, escorted by his relatives and friends, would visit the relatives of the woman's side to introduce his line of clan and relatives.

In the event of a divorce, which was common in Buganda, the dowry would be repaid. The amount depended on the length of time the wife had stayed married and whether she had any children within marriage. But today young people are often allowed to make their choice of partners, and arranged marriages are less common.

POLYGAMY

Among some of the other rural tribes today, marriage is also polygamous, and marriages are still arranged by the parents. The boy is usually consulted, and sometimes, the consent of the girl is required too, but often marriage is arranged by both sets of parents without the consent of the boy or the girl. Families often choose children's spouses early in life (normally when the boy is initiated), and some cultures demanded that all unmarried girls be virgins. Having a child before marriage was frowned on, but divorce was usually acceptable.

Among the Bakiga tribes it was forbidden to sell any animals given as wedding presents. Such animals could be used only to obtain wives for the bride's brothers or father.

In the past, tribal groups had other forms of marriage that were also socially acceptable. *Gufata* was a type of forced marriage, in which the boy physically carried away the girl. Another method was that boys of the same age would identify a particular girl and forcefully carry her to the home of the particular boy who desired her for marriage. When the boy slept with her, she became his wife, and further arrangements would then be made with the girl's parents. The reverse of this was *ukwijana* (ook-wee-JA-na), when a girl would sneak away from her parents and go to the boy's home to get married. If a husband died, sometimes one of his brothers would take on his responsibilities, including his wives.

CUSTOMS OF DEATH

There are still a great number of superstitions attached to death among Ugandan tribes. Burial was usually after five days, after which there was a month of mourning. Ten days after the period of mourning there would be funeral rites known as *okwabya olumbe* (ok-wa-by-YA o-LOOM-bay), an important ceremony to which all clan elders and relatives were invited. Events included eating, drinking, dancing, and the installation of an heir. The heir would then take on the responsibilities of the deceased if he was the head of a family. In the same ceremony other cultural events would take place, such as *okwalula abaana* (ok-wa-loo-LA ah-BA-na), in which children would be formally identified as belonging to the clan and given clan names (this is why in many cases Baganda have more than two names).

The Banyankole believed death was attributed to sorcery, misfortune, and the spite of neighbors. The body remained in the house for as long as it took the relatives to gather before it was buried. During the days of mourning, neighbors and relatives remained at the home of the deceased. No digging or other manual work was to be done, as a consolation to the relatives of the deceased, similar to the Baganda custom.

The Basoga had complicated death and burial rites. The process depended on the status of the dead. A chief was buried in the hut of his first wife with some of his belongings. The grave of a head of a family was dug in his own hut, garden, or courtyard, and an heir could be appointed at the time of burial. A childless man was despised in society, and his name was not given to any children in the clan. A married woman was buried in a banana plantation. The relatives of the deceased were obligated to bring another unmarried girl for the widower. She became the heiress and took over the functions and property of the dead woman.

Other tribes followed similar customs, but with some variations. For instance, among the Banyole when a man died, there were three days of mourning, during which there would be no bathing. If the dead person was a woman, the mourning would last four days. Among the Bagwe, if someone died everyone was expected to weep loudly; anyone who did not would be suspected of causing the death.

The Bunyoro feared death very much, as it was usually attributed to sorcerers, ghosts, and other malevolent nonhuman agents. Sometimes death was thought to be caused by the actions of bad neighbors, gossip, or slander. Burial took place in the morning or the afternoon.

BURIAL PLACES

In the area surrounding Kampala, which was for many years the tribal capital of Buganda, many of the former kings have burial places that can be visited. The best-known of these are the Kasubi Tombs within the city of Kampala, where four revered *kabakas*, Mutesa I, Mwanga II, Daudi Chwa, and Mutesa II, are buried. This historic site was once the center of the Buganda kingdom.

The Kasubi Tombs rank among the finest monuments in the Kampala area and are an outstanding example of the traditional skills and craftsmanship of the Baganda in building and architecture.

OTHER HISTORICAL SITES

Kabarega's tomb is another historical site. Kabarega was the ruler of the Bunyoro from 1869 until the British exiled him in 1899. He returned to

Uganda in 1923 and died at Jinja. The Karambi Tombs in Kabarole are the tombs of two kings, Daudi Kasagama Kyebambe (Kasagama) and George Kamurasi Rukidi II. The kingdom of Toro arose in the early 19th century when Prince Kaboyo, son of the ruler of Bunyoro Daudi Kyebambe, rebelled against his father.

Kalema's Prison Ditch, 10 miles (16 km) west of Kampala, is another burial ground. Buganda *kabaka* Kalema had 30 close relatives killed in this ditch in the late 19th century. The year 1888 was a year of political instability, as brothers Mwanga, Kalema, and Kiweewa struggled for power amidst the influence of missionaries and Arabs. The Muslim king Kalema had a ditch, 13 feet (4 m) deep and surrounded with impenetrable thorn bushes, built as a prison to hold his Christian brothers and sisters, whom he feared would mount a coup against him. The captured princes and princesses were brutally murdered and burned inside the ditch. They included Kiweewa, whom Kalema had overthrown just a few months before.

Some Baganda people did not believe that death was a natural consequence, and so, all deaths were attributed to supernatural spirits.

Four of Uganda's kings are buried in the thatched Kasubi Tombs.

UNUSUAL MOURNING RITUALS

When anyone died in the Japadhola culture, the corpse would remain overnight in the house in the exact spot where it had been found. Everyone who lived in the house camped outside, and none of them were allowed to bathe for at least three days.

EDUCATION

Prior to colonization, children in Uganda learned via what the Europeans described as "informal education." There were no defined institutions of learning, no trained teachers, no blackboards, no pencils and books, but children were taught all the same. In all the tribal societies, the system of education tended to be similar; only the subject matter or syllabus differed according to the particular needs and social values of the given society. Through stories, tales, and riddles, the mother or the grandmother would

An elementary school class in session in Kampala.

alert the children to what society expected of them as they grew up. The fathers would, through proverbs, stories, and direct instruction, teach their young sons their expected role in society.

Education was not confined to discipline; it was considered an all-around process that catered to all facets of the individual. Everything that was taught was directed toward the creation of the ideal individual who would ably fit into the society in which he or she was born.

When the British arrived and colonized Uganda, the whole system of parents and elders educating and training the younger generations began to be discouraged. The arrival of missionaries and the establishment of missionary schools between 1840 and 1900 changed the education system. The first mission schools introduced formal education in which the emphasis was on writing, reading, and religion. All schools were operated by missions until 1922, when the British government assumed some responsibility for education by

Trainee nurses attending class at the Lacor Nurse Training School.

opening the first government technical school at Makerere (now Makerere University), emphasizing the liberal arts and sciences.

THE EDUCATION MODEL

Unfortunately the education system in Uganda suffered extensively during the long period of civil unrest, and not everyone was able to go to school. In 1990 adult literacy nationwide was estimated at 50 percent. Improving this ratio was important to the government. In order to reestablish the national priority on education, the government focused on restoring buildings, establishing minimal conditions for instruction, and improving the efficiency and quality of education through teacher training and curriculum upgrading. The government also passed the Universal Education Bill, which ensured that every Ugandan child was in school by 2003 and received a good education. Happily the literacy rate began picking up and was 70 percent in 2006. Today the Ugandan education system is based on a four-tier model, with seven years of elementary education followed by a four-year high school certificate. This leads to a two-year higher education certificate, a mandatory requirement for entry into a university, where a basic degree takes three years to complete. Some wealthy Ugandans choose to study for a degree abroad.

Most Ugandan students have to wear a uniform.

UGANDA TODAY

Modern Uganda is, on the surface, quite different from the kingdoms that preceded it, although in many rural areas, life goes on in much the same way as it has done for hundreds of years.

It is in the Ugandan cities where the change from old to new is most obvious. In the traditional villages many generations of one family lived together—or close by—as a tightly knit unit that provided assistance and support to anyone in the family who needed it. With many people moving to cities to find work in the past few decades, families have often been split up, with the result that traditional support systems, especially for the young, no longer exist. This has led to problems such as a rising crime rate among young people. They no longer want to live the way their grandparents did but want to support themselves independently of their families—often in a society where work for the young increasingly demands the kind of education and training that few young Ugandans can afford.

The result is an ever-increasing gap between the rich and the poor in modern Uganda. This in turn fuels dissatisfaction among many people who feel that their future is blocked by the society in which they have been born.

But perhaps the biggest problem of all is political instability caused by the greed of the political leaders with lengthened term limits, who change constitutions to meet their own needs, which coupled with the belief in animism (belief in spirits) by Ugandans hinders the country's progress.

KNOWING THE RIGHT PEOPLE

Bribery and corruption are still evident in the way things are accomplished. It is sometimes easier to pass a little money under the table to get the license that you need than to work for it, and getting things done is sometimes not a matter of getting prepared as much as knowing how to influence the right people to make things easy for you.

Similarly, sometimes the easiest way to get a good job is to be related to someone with sufficient influence to get you what you want—which means that even those who have worked hard to qualify for a well-paying position sometimes do not get it because someone's brother, nephew, or niece is given preference in hiring. It is also not uncommon to get a job by paying someone to give it to you!

With an annual growth rate of nearly 2.7 percent, Uganda's population is set to double in a little more than three decades. Today more than half of the population is under the age of 18.

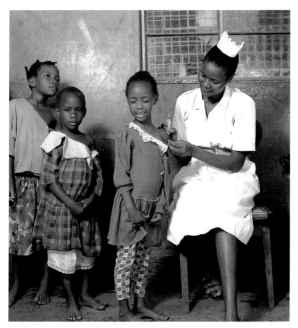

Health services in Uganda are available to all—though they are sometimes not as accessible in the rural areas as they are in the towns—and are provided by doctors, nurses, midwives, and health inspectors. Uganda's health spending accounts for 7.2 percent of its GDP.

Following the departure of expatriate professionals under the Amin regime in 1972, the quality of health care provided by the government declined, but it is slowly improving. In 1960 there was one doctor for every 15,050 inhabitants, but by 1980 that had fallen to one doctor for every 22,291 Ugandans. In 2008 the ratio was one doctor to every 15,000 inhabitants again. The problem is the lack of doctors in rural areas, as 80 percent of Uganda's doctors are in urban areas, yet 87 percent of the Ugandan population live in rural areas. A report issued in June 2009 stated that the health facilities across the country were in a sorry state and required immediate attention.

Disease is still a major problem in Uganda. Uganda was hit very hard by the outbreak of the HIV/AIDS epidemic in East Africa. In the early 1990s, 13 percent of Ugandan residents had HIV; happily this fell to 4.1 percent by the end of 2003, the most effective national response to AIDS of any African country. Same-day results for HIV tests and social marketing of condoms and self-treatment kits for sexually transmitted infections, backed up by sex education programs, have helped reduce very high HIV infection rates.

Malaria is the number-one killer disease in Uganda. Other easily transmissible diseases such as cholera and meningitis are still common, many of them caused by inadequate sanitation and poor hygiene. Diseases such as hookworm, venereal disease, and intestinal disorders are also common.

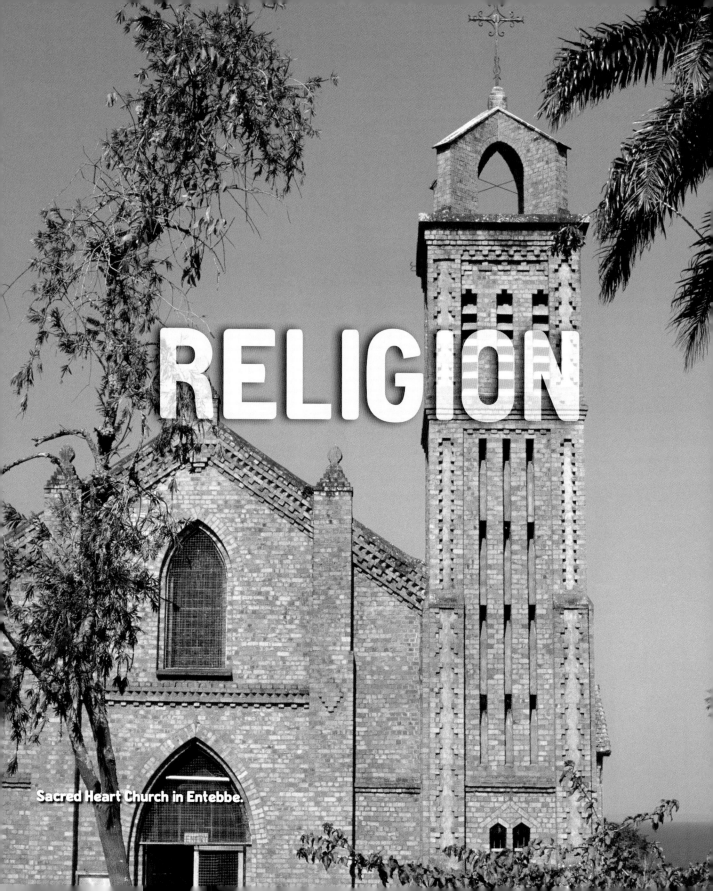

RELIGION

Sacred Heart Church in Entebbe.

LIKE MOST OTHER THINGS IN Uganda, religion was changed dramatically by Uganda becoming a British protectorate in the 19th century. Traditional religions, though still practiced, are less common today.

Religious tolerance, however, is an important part of present-day Uganda, where Christians, Muslims, Jews, and Hindus are all free to practice their own religion.

TRADITIONAL RELIGION

The Baganda believed that Katonda was the creator, the supreme being who created the heavens and earth. Katonda was also believed to be

Saint John's Church in Entebbe.

Before colonialism, most Ugandans believed in supreme beings. They also engaged in ancestral worship, believing that the spirits of their ancestors could influence the lives of those still on earth. With increased exposure to traders, businesspeople, and missionaries, many Ugandans adopted organized religion in favor of their traditional beliefs.

83

one of the superhuman spirits who took the form of a *mizimu* (mi-ZEE-moo), a *misambwa* (mi-SAM-bwa), or a *balubaale* (BA-loo-ba-lay).

The *mizimu* were believed to be the ghosts of dead people. When the body died, the soul would still exist as a *mizimu*. Such ghosts would haunt anyone the dead person held a grudge against. If the *mizimu* entered natural objects, such as stones or trees, the *mizimu* would become a *misambwa*, and at another level, a *mizimu* could also become a mythical tribal figure known as a *balubaale*.

Like the Baganda, the Basoga believed in a supreme being, Lubaale, and several other gods and subgods. Human beings worked as messengers of their ancestors, Lubaale, or other gods. To the Basoga, the spirit world, places of worship, animated objects, and fetishes all had power to do good or evil to the living.

JOK

The Acholi believed in a supreme being called Jok and in another god, Lubanga, who was the cause of evil. Lubanga had to be appeased at all times. The

Acholi dancers. The Acholi believed in a supreme being called Jok.

Acholi also worshiped the spirits of the dead and believed that they helped the surviving members of the family if they were treated well.

The Lugbara, the Langi, the Japadhola, and the Alur also regarded Jok as a supreme being. In addition, they believed in other gods known as the *jupa jogi* (joo-PA jo-GEE) and the *jupa jok* (joo-PA jok), as well as other spiritual entities and their dead ancestors. Worship was not routine but necessitated by misfortunes or diseases. In the case of a misfortune, the family head would approach a special diviner known as a *julam bira* (joo-LAM bee-RA), an *iolam wara* (eye-oh-LAM wa-RA), or an *ajoga* (eye-YO-ga) to have the cause of the misfortune diagnosed.

THE SPIRIT WORLD

The Basamia and the Bagwe believed in a supreme being and in ancestral spirits who intervened in human affairs and caused harm, death, and

Villagers performing a dance during a burial ceremony to ensure that the dead person's spirit will not attack them.

Each tribe had its own rules, and the young were taught the dos and don'ts of the society in which they were born. Among the Basamia, the Bagwe, the Baganda, and the Basoga, the taboos varied from clan to clan, but no one would eat the flesh of the animal that was considered to be his lucky totem. Parents were not allowed to sleep in the same hut as their son-in-law, and once children were considered adults, they would not sleep in the same hut as their parents.

Among the Bunyoro, pregnant women were not allowed to attend burials for fear that they might miscarry. Graves were marked with stones or iron rods so that nobody would build over them. If the graves were built over, it was believed that all the members of the family would fall ill and die.

misfortune if not appeased. Each family had an *indaro* (in-DA-ro), or shrine, where they would offer sacrifices to their ancestors.

The Bakonjo believed in two supreme beings, Kalisa and Nyabarika. Kalisa was half-man and half-monster. Nyabarika was believed to be the most powerful spirit being, with the ability to heal, kill, haunt, provide fertility or cause barrenness, and make hunting expeditions successful or not. Since the Bakonjo regarded hunting as a very important activity, both for sport and as a source of food, skilled hunters enjoyed a position of importance in their society.

The Bagisu had a strong belief in witchcraft, which colored their outlook on the most ordinary events. They also believed that their ancestral spirits controlled events, and so it was important to keep them happy, too.

MODERN-DAY RELIGION

The advent of colonialism and the introduction of foreign religions in the second half of the 19th century transformed the traditional cultures of Ugandan societies. With the introduction of Islam and Christianity, it became fashionable to communicate with God in Arabic, Latin, and English. The

Pupils in school reciting a prayer.

manner of worship changed greatly, as traditional shrines were replaced with mosques or churches with seats, organs, and electricity. Prayers became regular on Fridays for Muslims and on Sundays for Christians and no longer depended on particular instances of want or trouble. Organized religion gradually became a belief and a way of life.

Throughout Uganda's history, church membership has favorably influenced opportunities for education, employment, and social advancement, which may explain why today almost 84 percent of the population of Uganda is Christian. Sadly, a number of extremist cults have also sprung up in Uganda, and a cult calling itself the Movement for the Restoration of the Ten Commandments of God has been responsible for the deaths of 1,000 Ugandans.

MISSIONARIES

The arrival of the first Christian missionaries, Anglican and Catholic, took place in the kingdom of Buganda. Their message later spread to the rest of

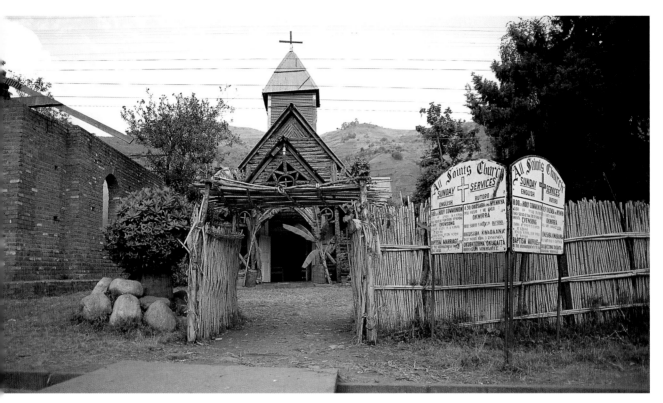

An old church in western Uganda that was built when missionaries first arrived.

what became Uganda. The introduction of Christianity set the stage for new developments and marked a turning point in the religious life of the people, particularly the Baganda, as well as in the political structure of the Buganda kingdom and the region at large. Christian beliefs and attitudes prompted a social revolution that was to transform all aspects of local people's lives. The events that followed, unpredictable as they were, added to the discomfort the changes had brought about.

CHRISTIANITY

Ugandans received the Christian religion with much excitement, but converting imposed requirements. As Christian doctrine denounced all native religious behavior and practices as heathen and satanic, becoming a Christian meant breaking away completely from one's old lifestyle and adjusting to new moral

A busy Sunday morning at Namirembe Cathedral.

and religious standards. New believers, called *abalokole* (ah-ba-LO-KO-li), were regarded as social rebels who had transferred their loyalty to a new religious system, thus turning their backs on the old tribal traditions.

With the backing of missionaries and their connections to the British government and its military might, Protestant and Roman Catholic converts were able to divide the Buganda kingdom, ruling it through a figurehead king dependent on their guns and goodwill. Thus the foreign religions disrupted, divided, and transformed the traditional state and made it easy prey for the ravages of imperialism that followed.

Nevertheless, the traditionalists fought back, and campaigns against Christian converts escalated, resulting in the execution of 26 Christians on June 3, 1886. Rather than deter the growth of Christianity, the martyrdom of these believers seemed to spark its growth. As has been observed in many other instances, the blood of Christian martyrs only helped to promote

In the early 1930s a breakaway group of Anglican missionaries together with several Ugandans initiated the *balokole* (BA-lo-ko-lee), or born-again revival, which spread throughout eastern Africa and beyond and has remained a powerful force of Pentecostalism in Uganda.

Christianity's foothold, and Christianity, in all its forms, is now the dominant faith in Uganda, although rivalry and even hostility between Catholics and Protestants is still alive. Some even say that the abstinence message preached by the Christian churches has contributed to the slowing of the AIDS epidemic in Uganda.

ISLAM

Although the majority of Ugandans today are Christians, there are still a number of people who follow the Muslim faith. Some Muslims are descendants of the early traders who came to Uganda before the arrival of Christianity, while others are immigrants from nearby countries where Islam is the main religion. Most major Ugandan cities have at least one mosque.

A mosque in Kampala.

JUDAISM

In eastern Uganda there is a community of Ugandans known as the Abayudaya who practice Judaism. They observe Jewish holidays and dietary laws, sing Hebrew songs, and keep the Sabbath holy, as Jews have for generations. This all started in the early part of the 20th century, when a well-known Baganda leader named Semei Kakungulu resisted both the European colonialists and the missionaries with whom he came into contact. Kakungulu read of the Jewish faith, met several European Jews working in the British protectorate, and was eager to read, learn, and practice. During the 1920s a European Jewish trader met Kakungulu and taught his community the theory and practice of the Jewish faith. In 1992 two Americans visited the Abayudaya for the Sabbath and were urged to send more visitors. Since then many more have visited the isolated community, including two rabbis and a delegation of American Jews. It is a very small population size, estimated in 2009 to number 1,100.

HINDUISM

A Hindu priest at one of the many Hindu temples in Kampala.

Most of Uganda's Hindus came from the Indian subcontinent to open stores and run businesses, which they did very successfully. Idi Amin subsequently expelled most of them in the 1970s. Their places of worship were not touched, however, and now that many of them have returned to Uganda, the Hindu temples are once again active places of worship and are an accepted part of the religious landscape of Uganda in the same way as the many Christian churches.

Children standing in front of a poster advocating education. English is one of two official languages in Uganda.

AS A COUNTRY WITH A multicultural society, Uganda is home to 38 spoken languages. However, there are just two official languages, English and Swahili.

English was introduced to the country only in the last century. Today half of the radio programs and newspapers are in English, which is also taught in all Ugandan elementary schools and is spoken in the courts of law.

English is not widely used outside of the major towns and cities, but access to economic and political power is almost impossible without

Considering that numerous ethnic groups are found in Uganda, it is no wonder that 38 languages can be heard. Uganda has two national languages: English and Swahili. English is essential for those in power, but Swahili is the language of the masses. Luganda is another widely spoken language, but mainly because of the Baganda majority who use it.

Students at an international school in Kampala, where children from different cultures study together.

having mastered it. Swahili is relatively widespread as a trade language and is the second national language of Uganda.

THE IMPORTANCE OF LUGANDA

Luganda is the second most widely spoken language in Uganda, after Swahili, as it is the language of the Baganda, the largest tribal group in the country. Luganda is spoken from the northwest shore of Lake Victoria and the Tanzanian border to Lake Kyoga, although mainly in Buganda Province, in the central and southeastern region.

Luganda developed over many centuries as a spoken language. It has existed in written form only since the arrival of the Arabs and Europeans in

During the regime of Idi Amin, Swahili became the second official national language, but it lost its official and national status in the 1995 constitution. In September 2005, the Ugandan parliament voted to once again make Swahili the second official national language.

Most shop signs in Uganda are written in English, a language that the majority of Ugandans can understand.

the latter part of the 19th century. At first Luganda did not have any standard spelling, which made it difficult to read. In 1947 a conference was held in Uganda to standardize the language. Now it has a clearly determined form based on five vowel sounds and 21 consonants. Luganda has both long and short consonant sounds, like the Japanese language.

OTHER LANGUAGES

The other languages spoken in Uganda are used mainly in local areas and sometimes for instruction in elementary schools; for government campaigns, such as birth control or literacy; and on radio programs created for people living in a specific area.

Among the tribal groups, languages include Lusoga, which is spoken by the Basoga, who live mainly between Lake Victoria and Lake Kyoga, and

Children read notices in English on a board in school. Sometimes other languages specific to an area are used in schools.

The native languages of the Ugandan people have had interesting effects on the English spoken in the country, leading to what many call Ugandan English. For instance, traditional Ugandan proverbs, clumsily translated, are often heard. A popular nontraditional one is a justification of official corruption: "Man eateth where he worketh."

Lugwere, spoken by the Bagwe people. Gwere is commonly used in the home in addition to being a medium of instruction in the first two years of elementary school. Acholi is spoken by 4 percent of the population, mainly in the north-central Acholi district, while Adhola is the most distinct of the Western Nilotic languages in Uganda.

Of the non-Ugandan languages, Hindi and Gujarati are commonly spoken among members of the Asian Hindu community that migrated to Uganda during the early part of the 20th century. It is also commonly used in newspapers and radio programs.

THE SIGNIFICANCE OF NAMES

Names are very important in Uganda, as they portray tribal and religious affiliations and sometimes signify what clan an individual belongs to. Due

In Uganda, tribal languages are still handed down from generation to generation, although English is the first language of many younger Ugandans.

Traditions in naming children are still very much alive in Uganda today.

to religious influences, however, most people in Uganda have an Arab or European name, which is more commonly used than their traditional name.

Traditional names vary from tribe to tribe. Just mentioning someone's name to a Ugandan is enough for him to know which tribe and what area of Uganda that person comes from.

The same names are often handed down from generation to generation. Sometimes chosen names are the names of gods or spirits, reflecting the traditional beliefs of the area in which the child was born. Circumstances prevailing in the tribe at the time of someone's birth can give rise to other names such as *Lutalo* (loo-TA-lo), meaning "war," or *Mirembe* (mee-REM-bay), meaning "peace."

Names can also relate to the appearance of the child at birth or wishes for what he or she will grow up to be, such as *Makula* (ma-KOO-la), which means "beauty." Most common of all is simply to call the child by the name of the day on which he was born, such as *Balaza* (ba-LA-za), meaning "Monday."

Multiple births give rise to special names, which vary from tribe to tribe. The Baganda, for instance, use *Babirye* and *Nakato* for girls, and *Wasswa* and *Kato* for boys. At the birth of twins it is quite common for the father and mother to take on new names too—the name *Nalongo* indicates the mother of twins, while the father would be called *Salongo*.

THE ROLE OF THE MEDIA

Uganda is a pioneer in the liberalization of the media in Africa. Private radio and television stations have mushroomed since the government loosened controls in 1993. Many people in Uganda own a radio, even in the villages, and listening to the radio is a popular pastime. Not nearly as many Ugandans own a television, however, as they are much more expensive. Sometimes villages will have a communal television set located in a common area—or owned by one person—and villagers will gather there in the evening after dinner to watch television together and discuss local and national events.

Both television and radio broadcasts have played a major role in raising public awareness of daily events and unacceptable practices such as corruption. In the past, many civilians were oblivious to the atrocities and corruption going on around them.

In Uganda there are now more than 150 radio stations, 69 percent of which cater to audiences in the country's 38 languages. Uganda Broadcasting Corporation (UBC) Radio, which is government-owned, operates five stations including commercial Star FM. BBC World Service is widely available, and Radio France Internationale broadcasts in the capital. Sanyu FM was Uganda's first private station, Central Broadcasting Service (CBS) is private and operated by the Buganda kingdom, and City FM is private and operated by the ruling party, the National Resistance Movement.

Television programs are on the air 24 hours a day, with programs mainly in English, Swahili, and Luganda. Digital satellite TV is now available in Uganda. UBC is the oldest television broadcaster in Uganda. National Television Uganda has detailed analysis of news in and around the country. Wavah Broadcasting Station (WBS), Pulse TV, and Nation TV (NTV) are other privately owned television stations.

The introduction of a free Internet service and a special Internet tariff countrywide helped to increase Internet usage, as has the recent strong growth of the fixed-line networks and an explosion of the number of cybercafes.

NEW VISION

There are four major national daily newspapers in Uganda, of which New Vision, the state-owned paper, has the largest circulation (about 35,000). It also publishes four regional subsidiary papers in local languages. Despite being owned by the state, it enjoys considerable independence and often publishes articles that criticize the government. The Daily Monitor and The Observer are the largest privately owned newspapers, the former having a circulation of about 25,000.

Uganda was one of the first countries in sub-Saharan Africa to gain full Internet connectivity. Both fixed-line operators, Uganda Telecom and MTN Uganda, offer a range of data services. Several Internet service providers are offering wireless broadband access. A new competition framework will liberalize Internet telephony completely, creating additional opportunities for the Internet service providers.

Cellular telephony has revolutionized Uganda's telecommunications industry since the first network went live in 1995, with two more following in 1998 and 2001. In 1999 Uganda became the first country on the continent where the number of mobile subscribers passed the number of fixed-line users, and the ratio is now more than 18 to 1. The market is consistently growing at around 50 percent per year, though market penetration is still low at less than 9 percent of the population.

ARTS

Villagers engaging in traditional crafts.

U GANDANS ARE VERY SKILLED in creating works of art, through performance and through practical skills. Some Ugandans excel in dancing and singing. Others are excellent craftspeople who make highly decorative mats, a variety of baskets, pots and chairs, spears, shields, bows and arrows, drums of various shapes and sizes, and other musical instruments.

Despite colonial rule, Ugandans have managed to retain their own art forms, as seen through dance and music.

DANCE

Traditional dances in Uganda are a way of celebrating events, and they differ from one tribe to another. The Karamojong jump high, while the Basoga and the Baganda use round movement of the hips much like Hawaiian hula dancers. The Ankole and the Bakiga have a very similar "cattle dance" that imitates the movement of their cherished long-horned cattle.

Right: Bark cloth is popular for making craft artifacts. Here bark is being stripped from a mutuba tree.

101

As with the prevalent cultures and languages, the similarities and/ or differences in the kind of dances found in Uganda usually indicate their regions of origin. To the unaccustomed eye, some dances seem to vary only minutely from region to region, yet a small difference in the performance can determine what occasion a dance signifies in participating cultures. Whether for marriage, birth, royalty, death, or circumcision, every type of dance was important and is still so today in many areas of Uganda.

The Baganda tribe has ceremonial dances such as *mbaga* (m-BAG-ah), *nankasa* (nan-KA-sa), and *olugunju* (o-loo-GOON-joo). The *mbaga* dance honors occasions such as weddings and royal gatherings, where the women and men often dance together in a choreographed manner. *Nankasa* is a popular dance performed on almost all occasions. The Bunyoro are famous for their *lunyege* (loon-YAY-gay) dance.

The Bagisu are famous for their circumcision dance, *embalu* (em-BAA-loo). The men dance in a circle around their friends about to enter manhood, while the women dance around the circle with encouraging comments of bravery. Most relatives take part in this lively and enthusiastic dance.

Drums play a vital role in traditional Ugandan dances.

ACHOLI DANCING

Acholi dancing is communal, and they have eight distinct types of dance—*bwola* (bwo-LA), *lalobaloba* (la-lo-ba-LO-ba), *otiti* (o-TEE-tee), *myel awal* (my-EL a-WAHL), *apiti* (a-PEE-tee), *labongo* (la-BON-go), *myel wanga* (my-EL wan-GA), and *atira* (a-TEE-ra). The *bwola* dance is the most important because it is the chief's dance and is performed only on his orders. The men form a large circle, and each carries a drum. The movement of their feet matches rhythmically with the beating of the drums. The women dance separately inside the circle without beating drums. The dance has a leader who moves by himself within the circle, setting the time and leading the singing. He is regarded as an important person and traditionally was among the few in the community allowed to wear a leopard skin.

In the *lalobaloba*, people dance in a circle, but no drums are used. The men form an outer ring, while the women form an inner circle. All the dancers carry sticks.

A dance group getting ready for a performance.

In the *otiti* dance, all the men carry spears and shields, and the dancers encircle drums that are usually attached to a post in the middle of the arena. There is more shouting than singing! The *myel awal* dance is a funeral dance during which the women wail around the grave, while the men dance the *lalobaloba* carrying their spears and shields.

Labongo is a dance following a successful hunt. Men and women face each other in two lines and jump up and down while clapping their hands. In the *myel wanga* dance, the men sit down and play their harps while the women dance the *apiti* (a women-only song and dance performed in a line) in front of them. The *atira* dance is now outdated, but it was held on the eve of a battle.

MUSIC

Musical instruments play an important role in Ugandan communities. The most popular musical instrument is the drum, which is used almost

Ugandan music is often a form of storytelling, especially in traditional songs. Traditional music uses lead singers with choruses that reply in unison, and it incorporates life issues and stories with morals at the end.

Drums are an integral part of Ugandan music.

Many Ugandan folk instruments are handcrafted using natural materials.

everywhere in Uganda. Music would be incomplete without the drum; it is used not only as a musical instrument but also as a form of communication, in dances and ceremonies, and for traditional worship and healing rituals.

The lyrics of traditional songs usually focus on loved ones, legends, daily incidents, or well-known events from the past. Songs are tuneful and accompanied by instruments such as drums, xylophones, shakers, logs, wind instruments, and string instruments.

FOREIGN INFLUENCES

Music adapted from that of other countries is common in urban areas and on many radio stations. Most popular is *lingala* (lin-GAA-la) music from neighboring Democratic Republic of the Congo, as well as West and South African music. Foreign artists performing soul, country, zouk, soca, reggae, rap, and calypso are also popular.

Most street markets have stalls selling audio equipment, blasting out music by bands from all over the world. Ugandans enjoy the emotion invoked by a rhythmic beat.

Professionals and intellectuals were targeted by the Obote and Amin regimes, and museums and galleries were looted and occupied, resulting in the destruction of numerous art collections.

There is a strong tradition of storytelling within many tribal groups in Uganda. The stories vary from group to group, but grandparents told the majority of the stories to their grandchildren as part of their education within the family. These stories have survived intact for centuries, and Ugandan children still love to listen to the elders of the family retelling these tales in the same manner they were told a generation before.

Although some of these stories are very old, they were not written down until quite recently, as none of the tribes had a written language. For this reason it is difficult to know how the stories started or what they originally referred to. Most of the stories that survive are directed at children, however, and have a moral. A great number of them feature talking animals. Some of these animals are good characters who help children, but others are designed to be frightening and warn the children of the consequences of behaving badly or of not being brave. Curiously, a bearlike creature (there are no bears in Uganda) is the main scary monster in some of these tales!

Two of the best-known stories are "Nabweteme" ("The Forest"), which shows the value of being courageous under difficult circumstances, and "Jogoli Jogoli" ("Disrespect"), which illustrates the importance of listening to the instructions of one's parents.

FINE ARTS

The practice and appreciation of fine arts are limited to a small but expanding section of the population. The School of Fine Arts at Makerere University has trained some of East Africa's leading painters, sculptors, and art teachers. The school also teaches industrial art and design.

African art styles are unique in their use of natural forms combined with a range of colors in tune with the lush vegetation and wildlife. It is a style less sophisticated than that of the Western art world but one that is growing in popularity and stature in galleries around the world.

Weaving is a popular trade, and locally produced crafts are common souvenirs for tourists.

TRADITIONAL CRAFTS

The traditional crafts that are part of Ugandan culture reflect the crafters' response to a variety of historical events and influences. Crafts have developed through the diverse traditions of the people and vary widely by ethnic settings. Simple handicrafts such as baskets and mats can tell a story and be identified with a particular tribe by the patterns they display. Many crafts are hereditary occupations in Uganda, and children learn skills and techniques while working alongside a parent or another adult. Certain clans are well known for specific crafts.

Ugandan crafts include making containers such as gourd and wood vessels, basketry, the weaving of mats and other house decorations, and furniture making.

Uganda's arts and crafts include the making of musical instruments such as drums, thumb pianos, lyre fiddles, and rattles.

LEISURE

A young boy plays with a wooden hoop in a village in the Gulu region.

LEISURE ACTIVITIES IN UGANDA ARE traditional, simple pastimes that can be enjoyed by most of the population. Some of the activities are Ugandan in origin; foreigners introduced others during the colonial period. The way people spend their leisure time depends on where they live, their position in society, and their economic circumstances.

Residents in rural villages, where homes may lack basic amenities such as electricity and running water, are more likely to spend their leisure

Ugandan girls playing a game using stones.

109

Two men playing *umweso*, a popular game in Uganda.

Storytelling is a
popular pastime in
Uganda. Children
love to sit and
listen while
adults recount
fables and stories
they remember
from their youth.
Traditional tales
have been adapted
over the years, but
the themes remain
unchanged. The
characters are
often animals,
and the stories
have a moral.

time visiting neighbors to chat or play simple traditional games. In villages where electricity is available, leisure options would also include listening to the radio or even watching television. Sometimes the gap between the poor and the rich is so wide in Uganda that one family could have a satellite television in their house while their immediate neighbor's home could lack even the basic amenities.

TRADITIONAL ENTERTAINMENT

Entertainment in Ugandan villages consists mostly of villagers sitting around and listening to the radio or congregating with their family members or fellow villagers to talk about their day and politics. Now with the proliferation of television sets, villagers might sit around enjoying the latest programs or sports on the village's common television.

TRADITIONAL GAMES

Ugandan children still enjoy the games their parents played when they were young, using little more than ropes, corncobs, or leaves. Wheel-rolling is played by opposing teams in the streets. The players stand opposite one another holding tanglers, made of two pieces of corncob on a long string. One of the players stands in the middle of the street and rolls a wheel down it, while other players try to stop the wheel with their tanglers. The player who stops it sings a song of triumph.

Some games are very simple. Dirt building is played by small children in a pile of dirt. Each child has a small red seed with a dark spot on it from an olasiti tree. A long pile of dirt is made, and the players hide their seeds in it. The pile is divided into several separate piles, and the opposing team guesses in which pile the seeds are hidden. All the other piles, except two, are scattered. If a team guesses correctly, it takes charge of the game. If not, this is counted as a score against them.

Ugandan children with homemade instruments, pretending to be a brass band.

FUN IN THE CITY

Town and city dwellers, especially those who are wealthy, have more choices than those who live in rural areas. Over the past few decades, and during times of peace, facilities have been built to accommodate those demanding a higher standard of recreation. These activities might include a visit to the movies, where international as well as African releases can be seen. There are also swimming pools and a few soccer stadiums, where local matches are held each weekend. Kampala now has a shopping mall, complete with a bowling alley, and an amusement park as well—Didi's World, Uganda's equivalent of Disneyland.

In urban areas the gap between the rich and the poor can be particularly wide. For the privileged few there is a choice of golf, tennis, or squash at members-only clubs. Municipal facilities are limited and outdated, so many prefer to entertain themselves at home. Children from poor families in

A family on their way home. It is not the norm for families to go out together in Uganda.

the towns use the same initiative as those living in the countryside and play traditional games together.

Going out as a family is not a Ugandan tradition—this idea has been imported from the Western world. It is still common, however, for women and children to go out on their own and the men to go out separately. Couples are normally seen together in the evenings. Many men tend to congregate in cafés and bars to talk and sometimes exchange gossip over tea, coffee, or alcohol.

Although food is important in Ugandan tradition, eating out is not nearly as common as having friends or family in for a meal at home. Restaurants are mainly for workers at lunchtime, for business meetings, or for visitors to the area.

The older people of the community have little need for modern forms of entertainment and are happy to sit and talk, discussing subjects such as politics, religion, and the family. Men and women of this age group usually sit separately in a social environment.

NIGHTLIFE

Urban evenings are filled with entertainment, with visits to discotheques and nightclubs, casinos, and movie theaters. This nighttime entertainment, however, is found only in the cities and large towns of Uganda.

Bars and nightclubs are filled with local dancers and live bands that often play until long past midnight. Traditional entertainers can also be found in the Kisenyi and Nakivubo areas of Kampala.

Young Ugandan men enjoying international music at a Kampala discotheque.

SPORTS

Many Ugandans are avid sportsmen and sportswomen. Boxing was especially popular in the 1970s during the dictatorship of Idi Amin, who was himself a boxer. During this period Uganda produced several world champions, and the sport attracted the uneducated and underprivileged and later spread to the high schools. Boxing has declined in popularity in recent years, partly because of the realization that injuries caused can be fatal.

Other popular sports include soccer, netball, swimming, tennis, golf, squash, rugby, and cricket.

SOCCER   Soccer, commonly known as football, is the favorite sport of Ugandans. It is played in schools, villages, and towns and at all levels of society. In the villages it is typically played as a friendly match between villagers, while in the towns matches tend to be between clubs, clans, or tribal groups. There are few soccer stadiums in Uganda, but players are happy to practice on any field or clearing around towns or homesteads.

Ugandan boys playing soccer in their free time.

Ugandan athletes have won a total of six medals at the Olympic Games.

Soccer is also popular as a spectator sport, and many Ugandan soccer fans watch international matches between top European teams on television. Young boys can often be seen wearing the colors of their favorite team.

NETBALL Netball is tremendously popular among schoolgirls in Uganda. The game is played with seven players on each team, and the aim is to get the ball in the opposing team's hoop as many times as possible. The netball court is divided by two lines, and at each end of the court is a shooting semicircle and a 10-foot (3-m) goalpost with no backboard. Scoring shots can be taken only from within this semicircle. Each team member has a designated position that is restricted to a specific area on the court. These restricted areas have both an attacking and a defending player in them, one from each opposing team. Many Ugandan girls with a natural agility and athletic ability for sprinting make good netball players.

A netball match at Makerere University.

Uganda's national soccer team is ranked 75 out of 195 countries in the world.

FESTIVALS

Ugandans performing during a festival
in Kampala.

>> THERE ARE MANY REASONS TO celebrate in Uganda. Some festivals commemorate traditional religious events, while others celebrate birthdays, wedding anniversaries, and graduation days.

Also important are religious festivals such as Christmas and Easter for Christians, and Eid al-Fitr and Eid al-Adha for Muslims. Traditional festivals are celebrated alongside modern-day ones, creating a fascinating calendar of events during the year.

The crucial stages of life—birth, puberty, marriage, death—have always been times of sacred importance to Ugandans, as they signify

Folk musicians perform at Independence Day celebrations.

Traditionally, Ugandans have considered each stage of a person's life as sacred and celebrated it as such. With the influence of other cultures, many other festivals are celebrated as well. Christian and Muslim festivals have been added to the Ugandan calendar. Other important holidays that are observed are secular ones such as Liberation Day and Independence Day.

117

Ugandans performing a dance during a festival.

changes in the status of an individual and that person's relationship with fellow members of his society. In rural areas these celebrations take on a traditional form, and most are unique to each tribe or area. In large towns and cities, however, festivities for these occasions have adopted a Western style.

BIRTH

The naming of a newborn child can take place at a variety of times after the birth, but it is always an important reason to celebrate. Sometimes a celebration is held immediately after the child's birth; other times it is held when all the relatives can get together for a party with plenty of food, singing, and dancing.

In Christian families the child is usually welcomed as a new member of the local church, as well as through the sacrament of baptism. This form of celebration, the contemporary christening ceremony, is performed regularly in Uganda for Christian families.

A woman with her baby. The naming of newborns is an important occasion for Ugandans.

DEATH

Death involves numerous customs. Customs surrounding funeral rites include playing mournful and sometimes joyful music, making speeches celebrating the life of the deceased, elaborate or simple embalming practices, and feasts of various kinds depending on the economic or social circumstances of the deceased or his next of kin.

FESTIVALS OF MARRIAGE

The rite of passage from the single to the married state is celebrated with many forms of festivals in Uganda. These ceremonies are often accompanied by feasting and gift-giving to express the pride of the community. The wedding festival welcomes the newlywed couple into successful participation in the community and its future expansion through the birth of children. Among most tribes, dancing and feasting after the wedding lasts until well into the following day. The food is simple—meat stew with rice or corn—but plentiful and is eaten outdoors.

In Uganda couples often have two ceremonies when they marry: a traditional wedding and a Western, Christian wedding.

Within certain tribes, it is customary to present large wedding gifts, such as the marital bed complete with new linen, pillows, and a bedspread, at the reception for the guests to admire.

Modern-day city weddings take the form of a religious service followed by a large reception for family and friends at home or at one of the many hotels in Kampala. This is a fairly formal occasion where a grand buffet is served to guests.

RELIGIOUS HOLIDAYS

The major Christian and Muslim religious holidays are celebrated in Uganda in traditional ways. At Christmas and Easter, Christians go to church and exchange gifts. Eid al-Fitr, which marks the end of a month of fasting, is the most important Muslim holiday and is celebrated by Uganda's Muslims with feasts. Eid al-Adha marks the end of the holy pilgrimage to Mecca.

There are few nationally recognized festivals in Uganda, but there are many minor festivals throughout the country such as those that celebrate harvests, the arts, and literacy.

A school band takes part in a Liberation Day parade.

SECULAR HOLIDAYS

Secular holidays in Uganda include

LIBERATION DAY (January 26), which celebrates the coming to power of the National Resistance Movement. On that day, the head of state gives a speech to the people on the successes and failures of the country to date.

NATIONAL INDEPENDENCE DAY (October 9) commemorates the day Uganda became a self-governing republic.

INTERNATIONAL LABOR DAY (May 1)

INTERNATIONAL WOMEN'S DAY (March 8)

Ugandan schoolchildren rehearse a play celebrating Uganda's independence.

Martyrs' Day, commemorated on June 3 by Christians in Uganda, marks the day when 45 Christian converts—22 Catholics and 23 Anglicans—were killed in 1886 at the orders of the *kabaka* of Buganda, Mwanga II, after they refused to denounce their faith.

FOOD

Fruit and vegetable stalls at the market in Virunga.

As with other
aspects of
Ugandan life,
colonialism
has changed
Ugandans'
eating habits.

BEFORE THE USE OF GAS AND electricity in Uganda, kitchens were often built separately from the main house. Cooking was done using primarily firewood, charcoal, or dung, so a separate hut for cooking kept fumes and smoke away from the main building. This is still the case in villages today.

In modern-day Ugandan houses, however, especially in the cities, kitchens are part of the main house and are complete with electrical appliances much like those in the West.

Although the food eaten by Ugandans today is similar to that eaten in Westernized countries in other parts of the world, in olden-day Uganda the kind of food that people ate depended very much on the tribal culture in which they lived. While some cultures had very similar staple foods, others differed depending on what was available and, more important, what was considered socially acceptable to eat.

TRIBAL FOOD

The staple foods cooked in a traditional Ugandan kitchen usually included meat (mainly from cattle

Right: Peanuts and fruit in a market.

and goats); fish; millet; sorghum; beans; berries of various kinds; potatoes; cassava; pumpkins; *matoke* (MA-toh-keh), a type of green banana; and milk products, such as cheese and curd. The Bahima and the Karimojong also used defibrinated, or baked, blood for food, as it was believed that some of the characteristics of the animal that it came from would pass into those who ate it, making them stronger or more powerful. This tradition is still practiced by some tribes.

A popular tribal food is *nyama chomo*, or roasted meat, which can be found in the restaurants and bars of Uganda today. *Oluwombo*, the Baganda way of wrapping stews in banana leaves and then steaming them, is also very popular.

COOKING IN THE OPEN AIR

In village homes, cooking was done mainly on open fires heated by animal dung, as this was the only fuel available. Cooking in the towns was often done in a similar way, but paraffin stoves are now used, as well as electricity

A boy cooking over an open wood fire. Electricity and gas are not readily available in Ugandan rural areas, so many people still depend on traditional forms of fuel.

and gas where available. Traditional cooking and eating utensils included huge bamboo storage baskets, winnowing trays, grinding stones, mortars and pestles, mixing ladles, an assortment of pots and dishes, calabashes, and gourds of all shapes and sizes, both to eat from and as mixing bowls.

Modern utensils are becoming common, but many Ugandans still eat using their hands, taking the food from a communal pot and using small saucers as dishes. Now that most Westernized packaged and processed foods are widely available, Ugandans have given up many of their traditional foods. However, they still enjoy eating local delicacies such as fried cassava, roasted sweet potatoes, steamed yams, and roasted corn.

FOOD RITUALS

Each tribe had certain rituals that had to be observed concerning what food could be eaten by whom and when. For instance, among the Karamojong, the meat from cows and goats was eaten only if the animals died naturally, not if they were killed for food. The Bambuti obtained most of their food by hunting, and they were very skilled at it. Among the Bagwe, women were not allowed to eat lungfish, chicken, and eggs, while among the Bunyoro, certain foods were reserved for particular functions, such as guest meals, which always consisted of millet and meat. Potatoes were never given to guests, except in times of scarcity, and in times of real scarcity, the Bahima could subsist on milk and blood.

Among the Iteso, the men did not eat with women but ate separately seated on stools, tree stumps, or stones. The women sat on mats in a circle around the food. Among the Basamia, the Bagwe, and the Banyole, women and girls ate together from the same plate, while boys and their fathers would also eat together. Unnecessary talking was not allowed at mealtimes.

WATER SUPPLY

The adequate supply of fresh, safe water to Ugandan villages and homesteads is an ongoing problem. Uganda still spends less than 1 percent of its GDP

In poor Ugandan homes the cook's aim is to provide as filling a meal as possible. Meat is expensive, so starchy foods, such as potatoes, cassava, and millet, are used generously. If meat is served at all, it is used sparingly to give some flavor to the other ingredients.

A SOCIAL OCCASION

Food is very important at social gatherings, and Ugandans will find any excuse to feast on good food. Communal eating is still held in high regard, so families and friends gather and eat together, mainly in homes. A relative or friend visiting after a long absence can expect celebrations with music and dancing as well as a table laden with food. On such occasions the food is rarely elaborate, but there is lots of it, and it is prepared with care. Other important occasions, such as christenings, holidays, birthdays, and anniversaries, all warrant a big celebratory feast for family and friends.

on water, and while 90 percent of the urban population has access to clean water, only 56 percent of the rural population does. Poor water quality has disastrous consequences. Stagnant water causes disease to spread rapidly within small communities and can endanger lives, especially those of young children.

Public awareness of the dangers of unclean water is growing, and the people living in rural Ugandan villages understand the need for an

A Ugandan boy fills up bottles with water at a water point.

MATOKE

Matoke is Uganda's national food and one of the oldest dishes in the world. It is popular in many parts of Uganda and is grown in almost every homestead in Buganda. When the matoke *fruit is ready, the leaves are cut off and kept for cooking, together with the plant fibers, which are used to tie the leaves together during cooking. The stalks are put in the saucepan too, together with the leaves, to ease the steaming process.*

To cook matoke:
Peel off the green skin of the fruit. Place the white flesh in the leaves and tie up with leaf fibers.

Put the stalk, some ribs from the leaves, and the bundled matoke *into the bottom of a large saucepan with more leaves. Steam for about an hour. Then remove the bundle and mold the* matoke *while it is still inside the leaves.*

Put the matoke *back in the saucepan and onto the fire to enhance the flavor. When the* matoke *is ready it will turn yellow.* Matoke *can be eaten with many sauces, stews, curries, and vegetables.*

improvement in the standard of the water they have been using. In the past, if the nearest freshwater supply was a few miles away, women would make the trip in an attempt to protect themselves and their children from disease. This chore would be repeated daily, in order to feed the demands of the family. In many towns and villages today this is unnecessary, as an increasing number of villages have one or more wells with a constant supply of clean water. Projects have been set up by charities worldwide to supply expert manpower, in the form of engineers and geologists, and funding to build these freshwater wells throughout the country.

COOKING FOR THE MASSES

In the less sophisticated Ugandan kitchens, food is often prepared in quantities sufficient to feed a large extended family or several smaller families within one community. The staples of potatoes, cassava, *matoke*,

Central and western Uganda staple foods are *matoke*, beans, sweet potatoes, and ground peanut sauce. Eastern and northern Uganda staples are millet and corn.

and beans form the basis of most main meals and can be cooked slowly well ahead of time and left simmering while the family is out working.

There is little variety in the daily menu prepared in a Ugandan kitchen—breakfast, lunch, and the evening meal often closely resemble one another. The selection depends on what is available at the market or what fish or meat the male family members have been able to catch that day.

Babies are introduced to solid foods at an early age, and soft foods such as boiled *matoke* and cassava mashed up with milk and sugarcane juice provide a balance of healthy nutrients.

DRINKS

In addition to milk and water, which are now obtained quite easily in many villages, most tribes brewed some form of beer that they drank with their meals. The Baganda made an alcoholic beer from bananas called *mwenge bigere* (m-wen-GAY bee-GER-ay), and a nonalcoholic type called *omubisi* (om-oo-BEE-see). The Bakiga made an alcoholic beer from sorghum called *omuranba* (om-oo-RAN-ba), while the Bahutu called their sorghum-based beer *amarwa* (ah-MAR-wa). Different types of beer are still popular in Uganda today.

Nonalcoholic carbonated drinks imported from the West are available, but more popular are the local, cheaper alternatives.

FRUITS AND VEGETABLES

A vast array of tropical fruits are available in Uganda, thanks to the lush vegetation growing high in the mountains throughout the country. Markets are held in most villages every day. Local women gather there to make their selection from the range of fresh produce on display. It is a social event as much as a domestic necessity and provides an opportunity for interaction with neighbors.

Tomatoes, avocados, citrus fruits, *matoke*, and many root vegetables form part of a healthy, balanced diet. Rural tribes living in the savannas

FOOD CRISIS IN UGANDA

Food shortages in parts of Uganda are approaching crisis level, as subsistence farmers have sold their produce for cash. Farmers were attracted by high prices of food products in neighboring southern Sudan to sell whatever food they had produced, leaving themselves with nothing to eat. The situation has not been helped by a long drought that began in November 2008. The Karamoja region, in northeastern Uganda, is the hardest-hit area , as it has suffered three consecutive years of drought, leaving up to 85 percent of the population in a state of famine. The government and the United Nations' World Food Programme distributed emergency relief food to the worst-hit districts in Uganda in 2009. Ugandans whose main crop of sorghum has been scorched have been living on wild leaves, ants, and mangoes. Nineteen percent of Uganda's population is undernourished, and not surprisingly, the country's global hunger index ranking is high.

of Uganda traditionally based their diet solely on meat. Today, however, improved transportation and communications systems mean that every market has access to a supply of fresh fruits and vegetables, provided one can afford them.

BUNYORO STEW

1 pound (454 g) beef, cut in 1-inch cubes

Salt, to taste

2 onions, minced

2 tablespoons (30 ml) butter or oil

4 tomatoes, peeled and diced

1 teaspoon (5 ml) curry powder

In a stewing pan, add just enough water to cover the meat. Season with salt and bring to a boil. Simmer for one hour. Remove the meat and drain. Keep the stock.

Sauté onions in butter or oil until golden brown. Add tomatoes and continue sautéing for five minutes. Add the meat and brown. Stir in curry powder. Continue cooking until flavors have blended. Add enough of the stock to make a stew of desired consistency.

CREAM OF PEANUT SOUP

2 tablespoons (30 ml) cornflour

24 fl oz (700 ml) milk

24 fl oz (700 ml) chicken stock

14 oz (400 g) peanuts, ground

2 tablespoons (30 ml) raw onion, finely minced

2 teaspoons (10 ml) salt

¼ teaspoon (1.25 ml) cayenne pepper

Put the cornflour in a deep pan and slowly stir the milk in, until smooth. Add in chicken stock, ground peanuts, onions, salt and cayenne pepper and bring the mixture to a boil, stirring all the while. Leave the mixture over medium heat for 5 minutes before whisking briskly. Strain soup to remove any remaining particles.

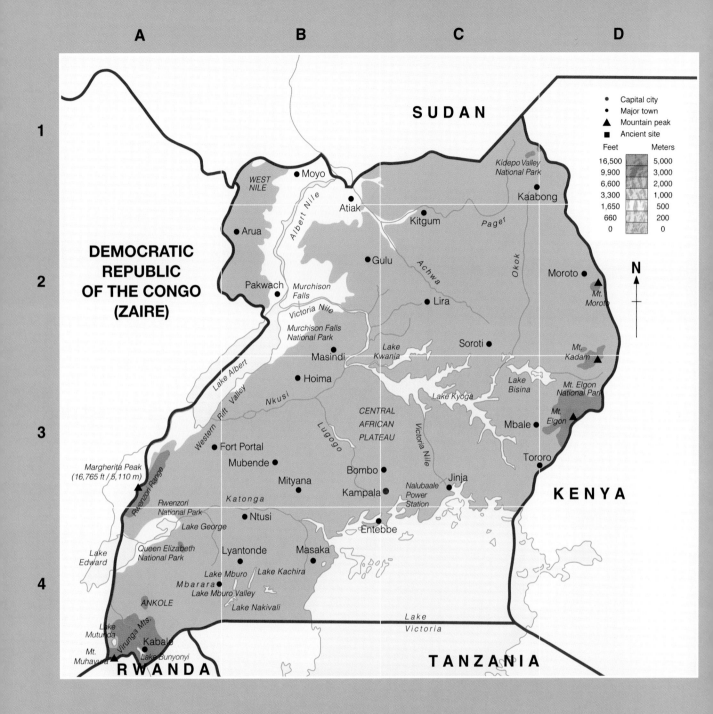

A   **B**   **C**   **D**

1

2

3

4

SUDAN

Kidepo Valley
National Park

● Moyo

WEST
NILE

Atiak

Kaabong

Kitgum

Pager

● Arua

Gulu

Achwa

Okok

Moroto ●

DEMOCRATIC
REPUBLIC
OF THE CONGO
(ZAIRE)

Albert Nile

Pakwach ●
Murchison
Falls

Lira

Mt.
Moroto

Victoria Nile

Murchison Falls
National Park

Lake
Kwania

Soroti ●

Mt.
Kadam

Masindi

Lake
Bisina

Mt. Elgon
National Park

Lake Albert

● Hoima

Nkusi

Lake Kyoga

Mbale ●

Mt.
Elgon

Western Rift Valley

Lugogo

CENTRAL
AFRICAN
PLATEAU

Tororo ●

● Fort Portal

Margherita Peak
(16,765 ft / 5,110 m)

Mubende ●

Mityana ●

Bombo ●

Jinja ●

Victoria Nile

KENYA

Rwenzori Range

Kampala ●

Nalubaale
Power
Station

Rwenzori
National Park

Katonga

● Ntusi

Lake George

Entebbe ●

Queen Elizabeth
National Park

Lyantonde ●

Masaka ●

Lake
Edward

Lake Mburo

Lake Kachira

Mbarara ●

Lake Mburo Valley

ANKOLE

Lake Nakivali

Lake
Victoria

Lake
Mutanda

Virunga Mts.

Kabale ●

Mt.
Muhavura

Lake Bunyonyi

RWANDA

TANZANIA

● Capital city
● Major town
▲ Mountain peak
■ Ancient site

Feet	Meters
16,500	5,000
9,900	3,000
6,600	2,000
3,300	1,000
1,650	500
660	200
0	0

N

MAP OF UGANDA

Achwa River, C2
Albert Nile, B1—B2
Ankole, A4
Arua, B2
Atiak, B1

Bombo, C3

Central African
    Plateau, B3, C3

Democratic
    Republic of the
    Congo (Zaire),
    A1—A4, B2

Entebbe, B4

Fort Portal, A3

Gulu, B2

Hoima, B3

Jinja, C3

Kaabong, C1
Kabale, A4
Kampala, C3
Katonga, B3
Kenya, D1—D4
Kidepo Valley
    National Park, C1
Kitgum, C2

Lake Albert, A3,
    B2—B3
Lake Bisina, C3, D3
Lake Bunyonyi, A4
Lake Edward, A4
Lake George, A4
Lake Kachira, B4
Lake Kwania,
    C2—C3
Lake Kyoga, C3
Lake Mburo, B4
Lake Mburo Valley,
    A4, B4
Lake Mutunda, A4
Lake Nakivali, B4
Lake Victoria, B4,
    C3—C4, D4
Lira, C2
Lugogo River, B3
Lyantonde, B4

Margherita Peak,
    A3
Masaka, B4
Masindi, B2
Mbale, C3
Mbarara, A4
Mityana, B3
Moroto, D2
Moyo, B1
Mount Elgon
    National Park,
    D3
Mount Elgon, D3

Mount Kadam, D3
Mount Moroto, D2
Mount Muhavura, A4
Mubende, B3
Murchinson Falls
    National Park, B2
Murchison Falls, B2

Nalubaale Power
    Station, C3
Nkusi River, A3, B3
Ntusi, B4

Okok River, C1—C2

Pager River, C1, D1
Pakwach, B2

Queen Elizabeth
    National Park, A4

Rwenzori Mountains
    National, A3—A4
Rwenzori Range,
    A3—A4

Rwanda, A4

Soroti, C2
Sudan, A1, B1, C1,
    D1

Tanzania, A4, B4,
    C4, D4
Tororo, C3, D3

Victoria Nile, C3
Virunga Mountains,
    A4

West Nile, B1
Western Rift Valley,
    A3, B3

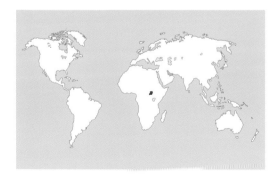

ECONOMIC UGANDA

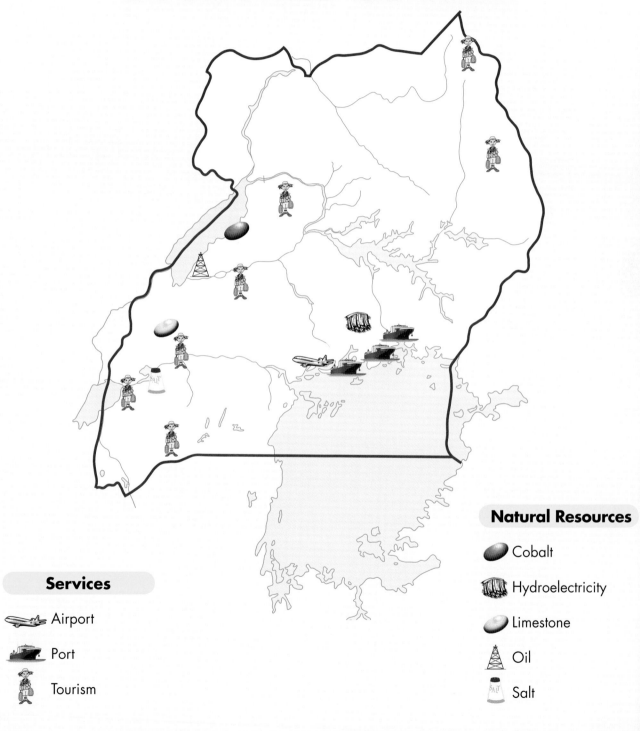

Services

- ✈ Airport
- 🚢 Port
- 🧍 Tourism

Natural Resources

- Cobalt
- Hydroelectricity
- Limestone
- Oil
- Salt

OVERVIEW

Uganda has substantial natural resources, including fertile soils, regular rainfall, and sizable mineral deposits of copper, cobalt, gold, and other minerals. Agriculture is the most important sector of the economy, employing more than 80 percent of the workforce. Coffee accounts for the bulk of export revenues. Since 1986, the government—with the support of foreign countries and international agencies—has acted to rehabilitate and stabilize the economy by undertaking currency reform, raising producer prices on export crops, increasing prices of petroleum products, and improving civil-service wages. The policy changes are especially aimed at dampening inflation and boosting production and export earnings. Growth continues to be solid, despite variability in the price of coffee. There has also been a consistent upturn in Uganda's export markets.

Gross Domestic Product (GDP)
$35.88 billion (2008 estimate)

GDP Growth
6.9 percent (2008 estimate)

Currency
Shilling
$1 = 2,053 shillings (July 2009)

Land Use
Arable land: 21.57 percent; permanent crops: 8.92 percent; protected areas (including national parks, forests, game reserves, and wetlands): 26.4 percent; other: 43.11 percent

Natural Resources
Copper, cobalt, hydropower, limestone, salt, arable land, oil

Agricultural Products
Coffee, tea, cotton, tobacco, cassava (tapioca), potatoes, corn, millet, legumes, cut flowers, beef, goat meat, milk, poultry

Major Exports
Coffee, fish and fish products, tea, cotton, flowers, horticultural products, gold

Major Imports
Capital equipment, vehicles, petroleum, medical supplies, grains

Main Trade Partners
Kenya, the Netherlands, Belgium, Germany, France, Rwanda, China, United Arab Emirates, South Africa, India, Japan

Workforce
9.8 million

Unemployment Rate
3.5 percent

Inflation
10.5 percent (2008 estimate)

External Debt
$1.705 billion (December 2008 estimate)

CULTURAL UGANDA

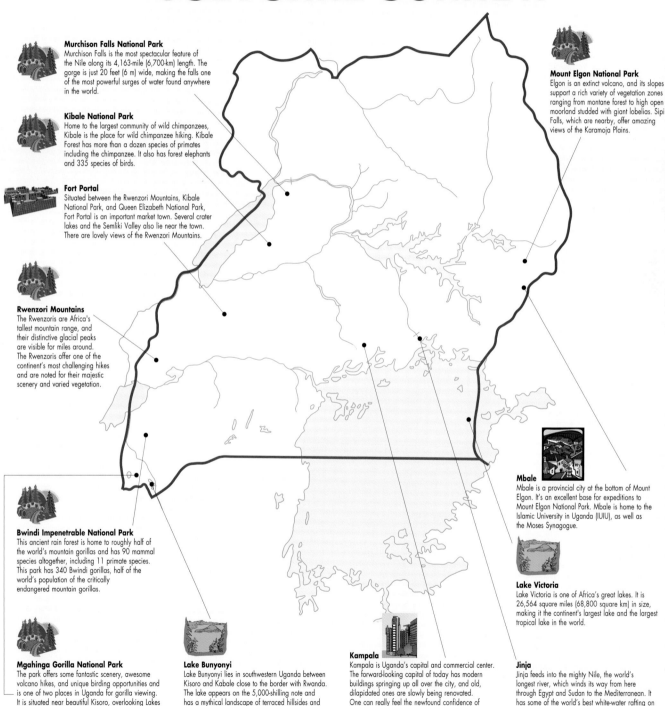

Murchison Falls National Park
Murchison Falls is the most spectacular feature of the Nile along its 4,163-mile (6,700-km) length. The gorge is just 20 feet (6 m) wide, making the falls one of the most powerful surges of water found anywhere in the world.

Kibale National Park
Home to the largest community of wild chimpanzees, Kibale is the place for wild chimpanzee hiking. Kibale Forest has more than a dozen species of primates including the chimpanzee. It also has forest elephants and 335 species of birds.

Fort Portal
Situated between the Rwenzori Mountains, Kibale National Park, and Queen Elizabeth National Park, Fort Portal is an important market town. Several crater lakes and the Semliki Valley also lie near the town. There are lovely views of the Rwenzori Mountains.

Rwenzori Mountains
The Rwenzoris are Africa's tallest mountain range, and their distinctive glacial peaks are visible for miles around. The Rwenzoris offer one of the continent's most challenging hikes and are noted for their majestic scenery and varied vegetation.

Mount Elgon National Park
Elgon is an extinct volcano, and its slopes support a rich variety of vegetation zones ranging from montane forest to high open moorland studded with giant lobelias. Sipi Falls, which are nearby, offer amazing views of the Karamoja Plains.

Mbale
Mbale is a provincial city at the bottom of Mount Elgon. It's an excellent base for expeditions to Mount Elgon National Park. Mbale is home to the Islamic University in Uganda (IUIU), as well as the Moses Synagogue.

Lake Victoria
Lake Victoria is one of Africa's great lakes. It is 26,564 square miles (68,800 square km) in size, making it the continent's largest lake and the largest tropical lake in the world.

Bwindi Impenetrable National Park
This ancient rain forest is home to roughly half of the world's mountain gorillas and has 90 mammal species altogether, including 11 primate species. This park has 340 Bwindi gorillas, half of the world's population of the critically endangered mountain gorillas.

Mgahinga Gorilla National Park
The park offers some fantastic scenery, awesome volcano hikes, and unique birding opportunities and is one of two places in Uganda for gorilla viewing. It is situated near beautiful Kisoro, overlooking Lakes Mutunda and Bunyonyi.

Lake Bunyonyi
Lake Bunyonyi lies in southwestern Uganda between Kisoro and Kabale close to the border with Rwanda. The lake appears on the 5,000-shilling note and has a mythical landscape of terraced hillsides and hidden bays.

Kampala
Kampala is Uganda's capital and commercial center. The forward-looking capital of today has modern buildings springing up all over the city, and old, dilapidated ones are slowly being renovated. One can really feel the newfound confidence of Uganda here.

Jinja
Jinja feeds into the mighty Nile, the world's longest river, which winds its way from here through Egypt and Sudan to the Mediterranean. It has some of the world's best white-water rafting on its doorstep.

ABOUT THE CULTURE

OFFICIAL NAME
Republic of Uganda

FLAG DESCRIPTION
Black, yellow, and red stripes that are repeated horizontally, with the national emblem, the crested crane, in the middle

TOTAL AREA
91,136 square miles (236,040 square km)

CAPITAL
Kampala

ETHNIC GROUPS
Baganda, 16.9 percent; Banyankole, 9.5 percent; Basoga, 8.4 percent; Bakiga, 6.9 percent; Iteso, 6.4 percent; Langi, 6.1 percent; Acholi, 4.7 percent; Bagisu, 4.6 percent; Lugbara, 4.2 percent; Bunyoro, 2.7 percent; others, 29.6 percent

RELIGION
Christianity, 83.9 percent (Roman Catholic, 41.9 percent; Anglican, 35.9 percent; Pentecostal, 4.6 percent; Seventh-day Adventist, 1.5 percent); Muslim, 12.1 percent; others, 3.1 percent; none, 0.9 percent

BIRTHRATE
48.15 births per 1,000 Ugandans (2008 estimate)

DEATH RATE
12.32 deaths per 1,000 Ugandans (2008 estimate)

AGE STRUCTURE
0—14 years: 50 percent; 15—64 years: 47.8 percent; 65 years and over: 2.2 percent (2008 estimate)

MAIN LANGUAGES
English and Swahili (official national languages), Luganda (most widely used of the Niger-Congo languages), other Niger-Congo languages, Nilo-Saharan languages

LITERACY
People aged 15 and above who can both read and write: 70 percent

LEADERS IN POLITICS
Milton Obote, President, 1962—71
Idi Amin Dada, President, 1971—79
Yusuf Kironde Lule, President, 1979
Godfrey Lukongwa Binaisa, President, 1979—80
Milton Obote, President, 1980—85
General Yoweri Kaguta Museveni, President, 1986—

TIME LINE

IN UGANDA	IN THE WORLD
	116–17 B.C. The Roman Empire reach its greatest extent, under Emperor Trajan (98–17 B.C.).
	1206–1368 Genghis Khan unifies the Mongols and starts conquest of the world. At its height, the Mongol Empire under Kublai Khan stretches from China to Persia and parts of Europe and Russia.
1500 Bito dynasties of Buganda, Bunyoro, and Ankole founded.	**1530** Beginning of transatlantic slave trade organized by the Portuguese in Africa.
1894 Uganda becomes a British protectorate.	**1789–99** The French Revolution
1900 Britain signs agreement with Buganda giving it autonomy.	**1914** World War I begins. **1939** World War II begins. **1945** The United States drops atomic bombs on Hiroshima and Nagasaki, Japan. World War II ends.
1958 Uganda is given internal self-government.	
1962 Uganda becomes independent.	
1963 Uganda becomes a republic.	
1966 Milton Obote ends Buganda's autonomy.	**1966** The Chinese Cultural Revolution
1971 Obote is toppled in coup led by Idi Amin.	
1976 Idi Amin declares himself president for life and claims parts of Kenya.	
1980 Milton Obote becomes president.	
1985 Obote is deposed in military coup.	

IN UGANDA	IN THE WORLD
1986 National Resistance Army rebels take Kampala and install Yoweri Museveni as president.	**1986** Nuclear power disaster at Chernobyl in Ukraine. **1991** Breakup of the Soviet Union
1996 Museveni is returned to office in Uganda's first direct presidential election.	**1997** Hong Kong is returned to China.
2001 East African Community (EAC) inaugurated.	**2001** Terrorists crash planes into New York, Washington, D.C., and Pennsylvania.
2004 The government and Lord's Resistance Army rebels hold their first face-to-face talks, but there is no breakthrough in ending the insurgency, which began in 2002.	**2004** Eleven Asian countries hit by giant tsunami, killing at least 225,000 people **2005** Hurricane Katrina devastates the Gulf Coast of the United States.
2006 President Museveni wins multiparty elections.	
2007 Uganda and the Democratic Republic of the Congo (DRC) agree to try defusing a border dispute.	
2008 LRA leader Joseph Kony fails to turn up for the signing of a peace agreement. Ugandan, Southern Sudanese, and DRC armies launch offensive against LRA bases.	**2008** Earthquake in Sichuan, China, kills 67,000 people.
2009 The LRA appeals for cease-fire in face of continuing offensive by regional countries. Ugandan army begins to withdraw from the DRC, where it had pursued LRA rebels.	**2009** Outbreak of flu virus H1N1 around the world

GLOSSARY

abasomi (ah-ba-SO-mee)
Converts to Christianity.

baami (BAA-mee)
Bagandan chiefs.

bakopi (BA-koh-pee)
Serfs in Bagandan society.

balangira (BA-lan-gee-ra)
Bagandan princess.

balokole (BA-lo-ko-lee)
Born again.

balubaale (BA-loo-ba-lay)
Ghosts of the dead believed by the Baganda to live in the form of mythical tribal figures.

homestead
Self-sufficient rural home with a plot of land to keep animals and grow crops.

indaro (in-DA-ro)
Religious shrine of the Basamia and the Bagwe.

kabaka (ka-BA-ka)
Tribal king.

kanzu (KAN-zoo)
Traditional Bagandan attire.

matrilineal
Inheriting or determining descent through the female line.

matoke (MA-toh-keh)
A type of green banana.

mbaga (m-BAG-ah)
Dance honoring occasions such as weddings and royal gatherings.

mirembe (mee-REM-bay)
Peace.

misambwa (mi-SAM-bwa)
Spirits of the dead living in the form of natural objects, such as trees or stones.

mizimu (mi-ZEE-moo)
Ghost of the dead believed by the Baganda to haunt living enemies of the dead person.

nalinya (na-leen-ya)
Royal sister.

namasole (NA-ma-so-lay)
Queen mother.

okwabya olumbe (ok-wa-by-YA o-LOOM-bay)
Funeral rites.

okwalula abaana (ok-wa-loo-LA ah-BA-na)
Ceremony in which children are given clan names.

okwanjula (ok-wan-JOO-la)
Formal introduction of the prospective husband and his family to the bride-to-be and her family before an arranged marriage.

ukwijana (ook-wee-JA-na)
The practice of a girl sneaking away from her parents and going to the boy's home to get married.

FOR FURTHER INFORMATION

BOOKS

Akallo, Grace and McDonnell, Faith J. H. *Girl Soldier: A Story of Hope for Northern Uganda's Children.*

Blauer, Ettagale and Laure, Jason. *Uganda (*Enchantment of the World, second series*).* New York: Scholastic Library Publishing, revised edition 2009.

Braun, Eric. *Uganda in Pictures (*Visual Geography, second series*).* Minneapolis: Lerner Publications, 2005.

Hattersley, Charles W. *Uganda by Pen and Camera.* BiblioBazaar; 2008.

Kubuitsile, Lauri . *Uganda (Africa).* Philadelphia: Mason Crest Publishers, 2004.

Oghojafor, Kingsley. *Uganda (*Countries of the World*).* New York: Gareth Stevens Publishing, 2004.

Otiso, Kefa M. *Culture and Customs of Uganda (*Culture and Customs of Africa*).* Westport, CT: Greenwood Press, 2006.

Sweikar, Michael. *Mzungu: A Notre Dame Student in Uganda.* Nashville: Cold Tree Press, 2007.

Tucker, Alfred R. *Eighteen Years in Uganda East Africa.* BiblioBazaar, 2009.

MUSIC

Benon and Vamposs. *I Know.* CreateSpace, 2008.

Magoola, Rachel. *Songs from the Source of the Nile.* Arc Music, October 2007.

O kello, Omega Bugembe. *Kiwomera Emmeeme.* Comin Atcha Distribution Group, 2008.

MOVIES

War Dance Velocity. Thinkfilm, 2008.

The Last King of Scotland. 20th Century Fox, 2007.

BIBLIOGRAPHY

BOOKS

Briggs, Philip. *Uganda*. Buckinghamshire, UK: Bradt Travel Guides, fifth edition, 2007.

Eichstaedt, Peter. *First Kill Your Family: Child Soldiers of Uganda and the Lord's Resistance Army*. Chicago: Lawrence Hill Books, 2009.

Finnström, Sverker. *Living with Bad Surroundings: War, History, and Everyday Moments in Northern Uganda* (The Cultures and Practice of Violence). Durham, NC: Duke University Press, 2008.

Fitzpatrick, Mary. *Lonely Planet East Africa*. Victoria, Australia: Lonely Planet, eighth edition, 2009.

Hanson, Thor. *The Impenetrable Forest: My Gorilla Years in Uganda*. 1500 Books, revised edition, 2008.

Leggett, Ian. *Uganda* (Oxfam Country Profiles Series). Oxford, UK: Oxfam Publishing, 2001.

Sweikar, Michael. *Mzungu: A Notre Dame Student in Uganda*. Nashville: Cold Tree Press, 2007.

Wade, Therone. *Encounter Uganda*. Longwood, FL: Xulon Press, 2007.

WEBSITES

Agreement on the Conservation of Gorillas and their Habitats. www.naturalsciences.be/science/projects/gorilla.

All Africa: Environment Body Lists Top Lake Polluters. http://allafrica.com/stories/200709260036.html.

BBC News Country Profile: Uganda. http://news.bbc.co.uk/2/hi/africa/country_profiles/1069166.stm.

CIA World Factbook. www.cia.gov/index.html.

CIA World Factbook: Country Comparison External Debt. www.cia.gov/library/publications/the-world-factbook/rankorder/2079rank.html?countryName=Uganda&countryCode=UG&regionCode=af#UG.

Domestic Waste Management in Kampala City. www.angelfire.com/nc/namicol/waste.html.

Globalis—Uganda. http://globalis.gvu.unu.edu/indicator_detail.cfm?IndicatorID=30&Country=UG.

The Guardian: Katine—It Starts with a Village. www.guardian.co.uk/katine.

Internet World Stats: Uganda. www.internetworldstats.com/af/ug.htm.

IRIN: The Fight Against Malaria—Uganda. www.irinnews.org/InDepthMain.aspx?InDepthId=10&ReportId=57927&Country=Yes.

Living Earth Uganda. www.livingearth.org.uk/africa_programmes/uganda/Plastic_Waste.html.

Mining in Uganda—Overview. www.mbendi.com/indy/ming/af/ug/p0005.htm.

Ministry of Tourism, Trade and Industry. www.mtti.go.ug/wildlife.php.

My Uganda. www.myuganda.co.ug/.

National Environment Management Authority Uganda. www.nemaug.org/.

Uganda Safari News: Uganda Conservationists to Tighten Forest Conservation Laws. http://ugandatravelguide.com/ugandanews/safaris/tours/uganda-conservationists-to-tighten-forest-conservation-laws/

Uganda Wildlife Authority. www.uwa.or.ug/.

Uganda: Women in Society. http://countrystudies.us/uganda/34.htm.

UNICEF Uganda Statistics. www.unicef.org/infobycountry/uganda_statistics.html.

INDEX

INDEX